AMERICANS
THE *Spirit* OF A *Nation*

DOLLEY MADISON

"The Enemy Cannot Frighten a Free People"

Zachary Kent

Enslow Publishers, Inc.
40 Industrial Road
Box 398
Berkeley Heights, NJ 07922
USA

http://www.enslow.com

Library of Congress Cataloging-in-Publication Data

Kent, Zachary.
    Dolley Madison : "The enemy cannot frighten a free people" / Zachary Kent.
        p. cm. — (Americans-the spirit of a nation)
    Summary: "Explores the life of Dolley Madison, including her Quaker childhood,
        her marriage to James Madison, her political life as First Lady, and her legacy
        in American history"—Provided by publisher.
    Includes bibliographical references and index.
    ISBN 978-0-7660-3356-6
        1. Madison, Dolley, 1768-1849—Juvenile literature. 2. Presidents' spouses—
    United States—Biography—Juvenile literature. I. Title.
    E342.1.K47 2010
    973.5'1092—dc22
    [B]
                                              2009030590

Printed in the United States of America

112009 Lake Book Manufacturing, Inc., Melrose Park, IL

10 9 8 7 6 5 4 3 2 1

To Our Readers:
We have done our best to make sure all Internet Addresses in this book were active
and appropriate when we went to press. However, the author and the publisher have
no control over and assume no liability for the material available on those Internet
sites or on other Web sites they may link to. Any comments or suggestions can be sent
by e-mail to comments@enslow.com or to the address on the back cover.

♻ Enslow Publishers, Inc., is committed to printing our books on recycled paper. The
paper in every book contains 10% to 30% post-consumer waste (PCW). The cover
board on the outside of each book contains 100% PCW. Our goal is to do our part to
help young people and the environment too!

Illustration Credits: Enslow Publishers, Inc., p. 47; The Granger Collection, New York,
pp. 10, 20, 27, 38, 41, 44, 51, 59, 67, 73, 76, 98; Courtesy of Kelly Nigro via Flickr™,
p. 112; Library of Congress, pp. 1, 4, 7, 12, 15, 17, 23, 25, 30, 34, 35, 55, 57, 69, 84,
87, 88, 105, 109; Courtesy of the Montpelier Foundation, pp. 90, 92; National Portrait
Gallery, Smithsonian Institution / Art Resource, NY, p. 9; © North Wind Picture
Archives, p. 81; Samantha Appleton / MAI / Landov, p. 63; © Shutterstock ®, pp. 100,
107.

Cover Illustration: Library of Congress (Portrait of Dolley Madison).

CONTENTS

This portrait of Dolley Madison is from an original painting by Gilbert Stuart.

1

The Escape From Washington

On August 24, 1814, Dolley Madison, the wife of President James Madison, stood at a window of the White House in Washington, D.C. She stared in amazement as people hurried along Pennsylvania Avenue. Horse hooves and wagon wheels raised great clouds of dust in the summer heat. Men, women, and children were crowded on carriages, carts, and wagons. They were trying to escape from the city. "People were running in every direction," one witness exclaimed.[1]

The United States was at war with Great Britain. Four thousand enemy British troops had landed at Benedict, Maryland, just forty miles away. These invaders were marching for the capital city, Washington.

President Madison was away with the American army in Maryland. Dolley had written in a letter to her sister, Anna, "My husband left me . . . to join General Winder. He [worried] whether I had the courage . . . to remain in the President's House until his return. . . . I have pressed as many cabinet papers into trunks as to fill one carriage [but] I am determined not to go myself until I see Mr Madison safe."[2]

From time to time, she climbed the stairs onto the roof of the White House. She steadied a large telescope on its legs and searched the distant roads for news. Most of her neighbors had fled. Even the one hundred troops that had been ordered to guard the White House had run away. The mayor of Washington, James H. Blake, had come twice to the White House. He had begged Dolley to escape the city. Still, she refused to leave without her husband.

Defeat at Bladensburg

Early in the afternoon, Dolley heard the booming of cannons miles away. At Bladensburg, Maryland, the Americans and the British were fighting. If the Americans lost the battle, nothing could keep the British from invading Washington. Dolley knew she must do something to save White House valuables. She ordered her carriage brought to the door and also a large wagon. She persuaded several men to help her load the wagon. Important government papers and White House books, silver, and china were packed aboard.

Dolley added to her letter to her sister, "Three O'clock. Will you believe it my Sister? We have had a battle . . . near Bladensburg, and I am still here within

President James Madison was with the American army in Maryland when the British invaded. Dolley Madison did not want to leave Washington until her husband returned.

sound of the cannon! Mr. Madison comes not; may God protect him!"[3]

James Madison's free black servant, James Smith, suddenly galloped on horseback into the White House yard. He had come directly from the battlefield. Smith waved his hat and shouted, "Clear out, clear out! General Armstrong has ordered a retreat."[4] He handed Dolley a note from her husband. The note explained that the British had broken through the American battle lines. The Americans had lost the fight and were retreating. Dolley worried that the British would take the president as a prisoner, if they caught him.

President Washington's Portrait

Several men had been urging Dolley to escape for hours, including local landowner Charles Carroll. Clearly, Dolley could not wait for her husband any longer. Before she would leave, however, there was one more thing she insisted on doing. A large portrait of President George Washington hung in the White House dining room. Artist Gilbert Stuart had painted it. It was so big and heavy that it was bolted to the wall instead of being hung from wires. Dolley later explained that her wish to keep the painting safe was out of "my respect for General Washington."[5] She felt sure that the British invaders would treat the painting with disrespect.

> "Save that picture, if possible; if not possible, destroy it."

Servants unscrewed the painting's frame from the wall. They lifted the painting down to the floor. "I have ordered the frame to be broken," Dolley explained in her letter, "and the canvas taken out."[6] Two New York businessmen, Jacob Barker and Robert G. L. DePeyster, just then arrived at the White House with a cart. "Save that picture," Dolley told them. "Save that picture, if possible; if not possible, destroy it."[7] She wanted to make sure the painting did not fall into enemy hands.

Gilbert Stuart painted this portrait of George Washington in 1796. This is the portrait that Dolley Madison saved as she fled the White House.

In this engraving, Dolley Madison is shown saving the portrait of George Washington. She left the White House only hours before the British arrived.

The two men took the painting to a safe hiding place in Maryland.

Brave Woman

"And now, dear sister," Dolley quickly ended her letter, "I must leave this house, or [become] a prisoner in it. . . . When I shall again write you, or where I shall be tomorrow, I cannot tell!!!"[8] A slave, Paul Jennings, remembered what happened next. "All then was confusion," Jennings declared. "Mrs. Madison ordered her carriage, and passing through the dining-room, caught up what silver she could crowd into her [handbag], and then jumped into the [carriage] with her servant girl Sukey."[9] Charles Carroll also took a seat. Only doorkeeper John Sioussat remained behind. Carriage driver Joe Bolin whipped the horses. The carriage hurried along the road out of the city.

Dolley Madison had made the position of the president's wife one of national importance. From the time she first entered the White House, she was one of the best-known people in the United States. Her charm and grace, her famous parties, and her impressive clothes were hard to forget. A woman of good will, sound thought, and extreme courage, Dolley Madison proved herself a valuable political help to her husband. The new capital city of Washington, D.C. became forever great during her time there. For her many services to her country, Dolley Madison rightfully holds a place among the founders and builders of the United States.

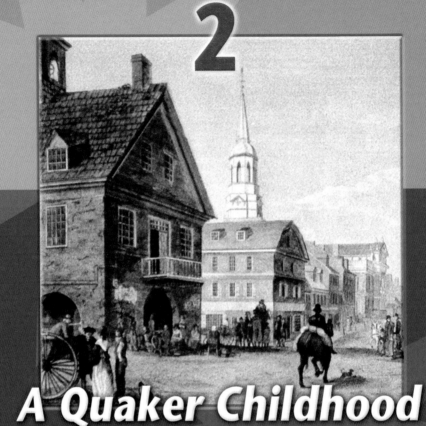

Chapter

2

A Quaker Childhood

"**M**y family are all Virginians except myself, who was born in N. Carolina," Dolley Madison once explained.[1] Her parents, John and Mary Payne, were members of the Society of Friends. This religious group was also known as the Quakers. The Quakers believed that every human life was special. They believed that God spoke to everyone directly and all people were equal. The Quakers put their faith in social justice and refused

George Fox and the Society of Friends

About 1650 in England, George Fox began preaching that all people had an "inner light." He founded the Society of Friends to spread his beliefs. Quaker religious meetings were times for spiritual thought. Any member was free to stand and speak on any subject during the meeting, if he or she felt moved to do so. Most meetings, though, were filled with long periods of thoughtful silence.

to carry weapons for fighting. Quakers lived simple lives. They addressed each other as "thee" or "thou" instead of "you", to avoid using titles of honor. Men did not remove their hats or bow to show respect to one another. Women did not curtsey or nod in greeting, as was common in the 1700s.

The New Garden Settlement

John and Mary Payne moved from Cedar Creek, Virginia, to North Carolina in 1766 with their baby son, Walter. Ten other Cedar Creek families traveled with them on the two-hundred-mile journey. In North Carolina, they would aid in establishing a new Quaker settlement called New Garden. A visitor described the New Garden settlement: "No spot on earth can be more beautiful," he declared, "[with its] gentle hills [and] excellent low lands."[2]

At New Garden, John Payne farmed land and also ran a store. Mary Payne gave birth to a second son named William in 1766. Then, two years later, on May 20, 1768, the Paynes had their third child. They named their baby daughter Dolley.

Dolley Payne was born in a log house. Today the location of the old Payne farmhouse is inside the city limits of Greensboro, North Carolina. "It was built of logs," a Greensboro citizen recalled, "had two large rooms, one a little larger than the other, with a huge rock chimney between them, with a fireplace in each room. . . . A stairway [led] to one big attic room for extra sleeping space and storage."[3]

Coles Hill

The Paynes did not stay in North Carolina long. In the early spring of 1769, they returned to Virginia. Dolley was less than a year old. Mary Payne had a cousin in Hanover County named Patrick Henry, who offered the Paynes the use of his farm, Scotchtown, for a year or two. In 1775, Patrick Henry would stand before the Virginia House of Burgesses and exclaim, "I know not what course others may take; but as for me, give me liberty or give me death." His support of the American Revolution would make him famous throughout the country.

By the fall of 1771, the Paynes had bought a farm of their own. It was a part of the Coles Hill plantation

Patrick Henry delivering his famous speech in front of the Virginia House of Burgesses in 1775. Dolley's family used Patrick Henry's farm, Scotchtown, for a couple of years.

owned by a cousin, William Coles, in Goochland County. The wooden house at Coles Hill was described as being "one of those low story-and-a-half Virginia houses."[4] There were sheds for tools and barns for storage, and a few cabins for black slaves. The Paynes joined the Cedar Creek Quaker Meeting House and continued farming. Their crops grew very successfully and their family grew, too. As the years passed, Isaac, Lucy, Anna, Mary, and John were born.

Farm Life

Little Dolley Payne grew up on a working farm. She rose with the sun and worked hard at her chores. She joined her mother and the kitchen slaves in cooking meals. She sewed clothes and tended the garden. She watched over her younger brothers and sisters. She probably learned household skills like the use of a spinning wheel to make yarn from wool. She sometimes sat up with the slaves when they were sick.

For fun, Quaker children were allowed to play with swings, kites, and jump ropes. Girls played with dolls and dollhouses. With scissors, they cut out paper dolls. They drew on slates and read poetry. But racing and card games were not allowed. There was also no singing, dancing, or music permitted in Quaker homes.

Dolley's parents taught her reading, writing, and arithmetic. In 1774, six-year-old Dolley attended a log schoolhouse near her home. Later, she entered the Quaker school held at the Cedar Creek Meeting House.

Freedom

Dolley Madison was eight years old in 1776. In July, news of the Declaration of Independence reached Cedar Creek. For years, many of the people in America's thirteen colonies had been growing angry. They claimed that Great Britain taxed and treated them unfairly. In April 1775, colonists and British soldiers clashed at Lexington and Concord in Massachusetts. Those battles marked the start of the Revolutionary War. Finally, the Second Continental Congress, meeting in Philadelphia, Pennsylvania, made a bold decision. With the Declaration of Independence, they declared the thirteen colonies had become a new, independent nation, the United States of America.

Great Britain would fight to keep its colonies. The Revolutionary War gripped the new nation. Victories at the Battle of Saratoga in 1777 and at the Battle of Yorktown in 1781 gave Americans hope they could win the war. Good Quakers, however, refused to carry weapons or fight. The Paynes' Virginia neighbors wondered if they supported the revolution or not.

John Payne had earlier written, "I am persuaded that liberty is the natural condition of all mankind."[5] A new Virginia law in 1782 allowed slave owners to free their slaves. Just six months after the signing of the Declaration of Independence, John Payne had freed

The Second Continental Congress meeting in Philadelphia on July 4, 1776, to sign the Declaration of Independence. Dolley was eight years old when America declared its independence.

one of his slaves, Cuffe. In 1783, he decided to free the rest of his fifty slaves. Most of his Quaker neighbors chose to free their slaves, too.

The Payne slaves were worth $25,000. When John Payne freed them, he got no money in return. He gave up their value and also lost his entire workforce. Without slaves, it was impossible for the Paynes to farm their land.

They had refused to fight in the war, and they had freed their slaves. As a result, the Paynes were scorned by many of their slaveholding neighbors. Unwelcome in Virginia, they decided to move. Pennsylvania had been granted to Quaker leader William Penn in 1681. Philadelphia, Pennsylvania, was called the "City of

Mother Amy

According to legend, Dolley Madison's childhood nurse was a slave woman, known as Mother Amy. Mother Amy refused to accept her freedom from the Paynes. She remained with the family when they moved to Philadelphia. She worked for the Paynes until her death. Mother Amy saved most of the money the Paynes paid her. When she died, she lovingly left five hundred dollars to Mary Payne in her will.

Brotherly Love."[6] This was because so many peaceful Quakers lived there. With twenty thousand citizens, it was one of the largest cities in North America. In the summer of 1783, John and Mary Payne and their eight children packed their belongings. They made the long journey to Philadelphia. The Revolutionary War had ended by this time with American victory. The United States had won its independence. Peace had returned to the young nation.

Exciting Philadelphia

Elizabeth and Henry Drinker lived on the corner of Front Street and Drinker's Alley. The Paynes stayed with these friends when they first arrived. Only weeks later, in the summer of 1783, Mary Payne gave birth to her last child. The Paynes named the baby Philadelphia Payne. Sadly, the little girl only lived until about the age of three.

In time, the Paynes bought a house of their own at 57 North Third Street. On the first floor of the house, John Payne started a new business. He manufactured laundry starch—a powder used to stiffen the collars and cuffs of gentlemen's shirts.

Dolley was fifteen years old when her family moved to Philadelphia. A new friend, Anthony Morris, recalled how "she came upon . . . Philadelphia, suddenly and unexpectedly [like] a summer sun, from the Sweet South."[7] In Philadelphia, Dolley explored busy streets filled with handsome brick buildings. Carpenters' Hall was where the Continental Congress first met. The State

The Payne family moved to Philadelphia in 1783. A Quaker leader, William Penn, founded the colony of Pennsylvania in 1681. This is an engraving of a Quaker meeting in Philadelphia.

House later became known as Independence Hall. The Declaration of Independence had been signed there. All around her was a city full of adventure and history.

In her plain gray Quaker dress and bonnet, Dolley gazed at citizens dressed in the latest fashions. She watched as they strolled on Chestnut Street and rode in their carriages beside the Delaware River. Dolley was a girl full of good cheer and energy. She sometimes visited friends in Haddonfield, New Jersey. It was one of the oldest Quaker towns in the region. People there remembered her as having an "oval face, a nose tilted like a flower, jet-black hair, and blue eyes. . . . Those beautiful eyes [excited] the hearts of the Quaker lads of Haddonfield."[8]

John Todd Jr.

By 1789, John Payne's starch business had failed. He could not sell enough starch to pay his expenses. Quakers frowned upon business failure. They believed only weak people allowed themselves to get into debt. Members of the Pine Street Meeting House suddenly refused to let John Payne attend services. Deeply depressed, Dolley's father remained in bed for days at a time. In shame, he refused to leave his room.

Dolley had grown into a beautiful, charming woman. She had many admirers. Her father thought she should marry a Quaker named John Todd Jr. The handsome young lawyer seemed a good match for Dolley. A friend, Sarah Parker, noted in December 1789, "Dolly Payne is likely to unite herself to a young

Writing a Constitution

In May 1787, a convention assembled at the State House in Philadelphia. Fifty-five delegates gathered to design a new American government. During months of serious debate, the delegates wrote the Constitution. That document describes the basic powers of the United States government. One of the convention leaders was James Madison of Virginia. Madison attended every session of the convention and spoke 161 times. South Carolina delegate Pierce Butler declared, "In the management of every great question he . . . took the lead in the Convention."[9]

man named J. Todd."[10] John Todd remained true to Dolley, even though her father's bad luck embarrassed the Payne family.

On the snowy day of January 7, 1790, Dolley Payne and John Todd Jr. married at the Pine Street Meeting House. Dolley was twenty-one years old and John Todd Jr. was twenty-six. Following Quaker custom, the two young people stood up in the meeting house. John Todd's wedding gift to Dolley was a small watercolor picture of himself. It was painted by Charles Willson Peale, one of America's leading artists at the time.

A view of Second Street North and Market Street in Philadelphia around 1800. Dolley enjoyed walking the streets of the city and gazing at the citizens in the latest fashions.

The Todd Home

Just one year after their marriage, John Todd bought a house on the corner of Fourth and Walnut Streets. It was a well-built house of red-and-black brick. It had a separate two-story brick kitchen and a wooden stable for their horses. The Todds and Dolley's sister, eleven-year-old Anna, settled in. The Todd house stood in one of Philadelphia's finest neighborhoods. Dolley's family lived only a few blocks away.

On October 24, 1792, John Payne died. Many people said Dolley's father had died of a broken heart. The shame of his business failure had been too much for him. In order to support her family, Mary Payne already had opened her home as a boardinghouse. People rented rooms, and she also served meals in her dining room. Boarders included congress members and government officials. The United States government had moved all of its offices from New York City to Philadelphia in 1790.

Dolley and John Todd seemed to have a loving, happy marriage. Their first child, John Payne Todd, was named after Dolley's husband and her father. Born in the Fourth Street house on February 29, 1792, they called him Payne. As she watched her baby boy grow, Dolley could not guess the horror that would soon grip Philadelphia.

3

The Great Little Madison

"There have been an unusual number of funerals lately here," wrote Dolley Todd's Philadelphia friend Elizabeth Drinker on August 16, 1793.[1] During the summer of 1793, yellow fever swept through the city. Fever, chills, headache, muscle aches, tiredness, and black vomit were signs of the deadly disease. Kidney and liver failure could turn a victim's skin yellow. Yellow fever could kill a person in just one day.

Many people thought the disease was caused by "bad air."[2] In truth, open sewers, puddles of standing water, and piles of rotting garbage gave mosquitoes places to live. It was the bite of the mosquito that caused the disease. Yellow fever could not be passed from person to person. At the time, most people feared that it could. When the fever broke out in 1793, Philadelphians fled the city. Almost half the population escaped into the countryside. The United States government moved to the town of Germantown. President George Washington moved into a rented house there with his family.

Gray's Ferry

By the end of August, Philadelphia gravediggers were burying twenty-four bodies each day. In the middle of the horrible yellow fever epidemic, Dolley gave birth to her second son. William Temple Todd was born in September 1793. The birth left both mother and child weak. Greatly worried, John Todd brought Dolley and their two children out of the city. He took them to Gray's Ferry, just across the Schuylkill River. He hoped the fever would not reach them there. Dolley's mother came along to take care of the baby. John Todd could not stay with his wife and children. He returned to the city to look after his law business and his parents.

In Philadelphia, John Todd's law clerk, Isaac Heston, remained at the Todd house. On September 19, Heston penned a letter to his brother: "All around us great are the numbers that are called to the grave. . . .

AT a MEETING of the Corporation of the city of Burlington, August 30th, 1793, the following recommendations to the citizens was unanimously agreed to.

WHEREAS there is great reason for caution against the malignant Fever or contagious disorder, which prevails in Philadelphia, and it is our duty to use every probable means to prevent the same in the city of Burlington; the Corporation of Burlington after collecting every advice which could be obtained,

RECOMMEND to the Citizens of Burlington,

1. That all unnecessary intercourse be avoided with Philadelphia, that no dry goods, woollen cloths, woollens, cottons or linens, or any packages where straw, hay or shavings are used, be imported within twenty days.

2. That the masters of the boats which ply to and from Burlington to Philadelphia, be very careful that they do not receive on board their vessels, or bring to this city within twenty days, any person or persons but those who appear in good health.

3. That no animal or vegetable substances be thrown or permitted to lay in the streets or alleys, but that all offals, water-melon rinds and substances that putrefy be thrown into the delaware or buried.

4. That no water be permitted to stagnate about the pumps, in the streets or near any houses; but that the wharves, streets, alleys and gutters, ditches, house, and barnyards, be kept as clean as possible.

5. The Physicians in Burlington are requested to make report to the Mayor or Recorder as soon as possible, after they shall have been called to and visited any person or persons, who shall have the said malignant Fever.

Signed by order of the Corporation,

BOWES REED, *Mayor.*

The following means to prevent the contagion is recommended by the College of Physicians in Philadelphia.

" To avoid all fatigue of body and mind."

" To avoid standing or setting in the sun, also in a current of air, or in the evening air."

" To accommodate the dress to the weather, and to exceed rather in warm than in cool cloathing."

" To avoid intemperance, but to use fermented liquors, such as wine, beer and cyder with moderation."

" The burning of gunpowder, the use of vinegar and camphor upon handkerchiefs or in smelling bottels, particularly by persons whose duty calls them to visit or attend the sick."

Published by order of the Corporation,

ABRAHAM GARDINER, *Clerk.*

Yellow fever swept through Philadelphia in 1793. This notice was printed to warn residents about the spread of the disease.

There is [hardly] anybody to be seen in many parts of the town."[3] Just ten days later, Heston died of the terrible fever. Next, Dolley's father-in-law John Todd Sr. died on October 2. John Todd Jr. was about to bring his mother to the country when she also died on October 12.

The Hand of Death

When her husband visited Gray's Ferry a few days later, Dolley begged him to stay with her. He promised he would as soon as he closed his office. On another visit, John Todd suddenly felt himself growing sick. To keep from passing the disease to Dolley and his children, he immediately went back to his brother's house in Philadelphia. It was there that John Todd Jr. died of yellow fever on October 24, 1793.

Just hours after her husband's death, yellow fever also killed Dolley's baby, William Temple. For the rest of her life, October was a month of painful sadness for Dolley. Mary Payne wrote in a letter, "My poor Dear Dolley, what does she . . . suffer."[4]

The yellow fever epidemic had claimed the lives of five thousand Philadelphians. That was nearly one fifth of the city's population. Dolley, her son Payne, and her sister Anna, returned to the house on Fourth and Walnut Street in December 1793. She was a widow, although she was not even twenty-five years old.

Aaron Burr

The cold winter months of 1793–1794 were very difficult for Dolley. She carried a heavy sadness in her heart.

Mary Payne's boardinghouse at 96 North Third Street attracted new boarders that winter. One of them was a young senator and lawyer from New York, Aaron Burr. Dolley grew to trust Burr. He helped Dolley take ownership of the property her husband had left her in his will.

By the spring of 1794, Dolley had begun to feel more cheerful. She went out in public more often. Even in her Quaker bonnet, she was easy to notice as she strolled along. Men stood in the Philadelphia streets just to get a look at the lovely Widow Todd. "Really, Dolley," her friend Elizabeth Collins once said with embarrassment, "thou must hide thy face, there are so many staring at thee."[5]

A beautiful widow was sure to attract gentlemen admirers. One of them was a congress member from Virginia, forty-three-year-old James Madison. He was already famous for his part in writing the Constitution and the Bill of Rights. Congress member Madison was greatly respected. President Washington even chose Madison to help write his 1789 inaugural address. Washington often relied on Madison's advice in governing the country.

A Social Introduction

In May 1794, Madison asked his friend Aaron Burr for help. He wanted to meet Dolley Todd. The two men were old friends. They had been classmates at the College of New Jersey (now Princeton University). One day, a messenger delivered a note to Dolley. The note would change her life. Aaron Burr asked for permission

Aaron Burr, pictured here, helped introduce James Madison to Dolley Todd in 1794.

to bring James Madison on a social call that evening. Excitedly, Dolley wrote to her friend Eliza Collins. "Friend," Dolley explained, "Thou must come to me. Aaron Burr says that the great little Madison has asked to be brought to see me this evening."[6]

That night, the two men knocked on the door at Widow Todd's house. There they were greeted by Dolley and her Quaker friend, Eliza Collins. Years later, Lucia Beverly Cutts, Dolley's grand-niece, described what Dolley wore that evening. "She was dressed in . . . satin, with a silk . . . kerchief over her neck . . . " On her head was "a cap, from which an occasional . . . curl would escape."[7] James Madison almost always dressed in a dark suit. Dolley's first cousin, Edward Coles, would recall, "I never knew him to wear any other color than black."[8] Madison usually wore powder on his hair. It was pulled back and tied in a queue like a ponytail. Madison was a small man, about five feet, four inches tall, a little shorter than Dolley.

Courtship

Madison's first visit to Dolley was a romantic success. Dolley's niece, Mary Cutts, later wrote that "she

A Broken Engagement

James Madison had been in love before he met Dolley Todd. In 1782, when he was thirty-one, he had asked fifteen-year-old Catherine "Kitty" Floyd to marry him. Teenage women often were married in the 1700s. She was the daughter of New York congress member William Floyd. Kitty Floyd, however, broke her engagement with Madison in July 1783. She had decided she would rather marry William Clarkson, a nineteen-year-old medical student.

conquered . . . Madison, who was considered an old bachelor."[9] Dolley did not fall in love immediately. She knew Madison had a good reputation. If she married him, she would gain wealth and social position. But Dolley was still a Quaker, and James Madison was an Episcopalian. If she married outside of her religion, the Quakers would almost surely expel Dolley. She carefully considered this important step.

Rumors of the romance soon reached the Philadelphia home of President and Mrs. Washington. Martha Washington invited Dolley to tea.

"[Dolley], is it true that you are engaged to James Madison?" she asked.

"No," Dolley quietly answered, "I think not."

"If it is so," Martha Washington continued, "do not be ashamed to confess it. Rather be proud. He will

> "To begin, he thinks so much of you in the Day that he has Lost his Tongue. At Night he Dreams of you."

make thee a good husband, and all the better for being so much older."[10] She and President Washington both approved of the relationship.

James Madison was certainly in love with her. In June 1794, Dolley's cousin Catherine Coles wrote Dolley a letter, "Now for Madison, he told me I might say what I pleased to you about him. To begin, he thinks so much of you in the Day that he has Lost his Tongue. At Night he Dreams of you."[11]

In the summer of 1794, Dolley rented out her house in Philadelphia. She traveled to Virginia to visit her sister Lucy, who had married George Steptoe Washington, President Washington's favorite nephew. They lived at an estate called Harewood. By letter, Madison proposed marriage. Dolley answered by letter and agreed to marry him. Madison was thrilled.

Marriage

Early in September, Madison and his twenty-year-old sister Fanny journeyed to Harewood. He presented Dolley with a beautiful engagement ring. The ring had a gold band and a large diamond surrounded by seven smaller ones.

On September 15, 1794, Dolley wrote to Eliza Collins, "In the course of this day I give my hand to the man who of all others I most admire."[12] In the large living room at Harewood, Dolley and James were married by Madison's cousin, the Reverend Alexander Balmaine.

Dolley's wedding gown was not a plain Quaker dress. The fancy dress of silk and lace had a low V-neck. The dress tightly fitted Dolley's waist. On her hair, she wore a wreath of orange blossoms. On her feet were white satin shoes with low heels. Perhaps she did not want to look taller than her new husband.

A Congress Member's Wife

Three months after her wedding, Dolley was expelled by the Society of Friends for not marrying a Quaker. At home, she still wore her plain Quaker clothes. In public, though, she began wearing colorful gowns and fancy shoes. She held dinner parties and attended dances. She gladly took up her social duties as a congress member's wife.

Dolley made a lasting impression on congress member Samuel L. Mitchill. He wrote of Madison's new bride, "Her smile, her conversation, and her manners are so engaging that it is no wonder that such a young widow, with her fine blue eyes . . . should indeed be a queen of hearts. By this second marriage she has become the wife of one of the first men of the nation . . . "[13]

Whenever Congress was in session, Dolley had to be ready to entertain. The ladies of Philadelphia society helped create the styles of America. Madison always looked upon his wife as his equal. At dinner parties, he asked that Dolley sit at the head of the table. He felt happiest letting her lead the table conversation.

Dolley and James Madison were married in this room at the Harewood estate.

Dolley had a talent for making guests feel relaxed and comfortable.

Vice President John Adams wrote to his wife Abigail, "My Dearest Friend.—I dined Yesterday with Mr. Madison. Mrs. Madison is a fine Woman."[14] When Abigail Adams came to Philadelphia, she learned about Dolley first hand. "An invitation to dine with Mrs. Madison," she admitted, "is prized by all who are asked to her home."[15] Congress member Charles Jared Ingersoll described one meal at the Madisons: "The table was . . . handsomely provided; good soups, [meat], fish, and vegetables, well cooked—dessert and excellent wine of various kinds."[16]

Dolley and James Madison lived at 429 Spruce Street. As time passed, people noticed that the

Madisons had not started a family of their own. Aaron Burr wrote to a friend, "Madison still childless—and I fear like to continue so."[17] Whatever the reason, both Dolley and James were deeply saddened that they could not have children. Dolley loved young people. She liked to spoil her son, Payne Todd, and always enjoyed visits from nieces and nephews.

Early Retirement

In 1796, John Adams was elected president. Eight years as president had been enough for George Washington. He had chosen not to run for office again. Forty-five-year-old James Madison had decided he would not run for congress again either. He gladly set aside his political career to retire. In the early spring of 1797, the Madisons closed their Philadelphia home. They packed their belongings. With five-year-old Payne Todd and Dolley's sister, eighteen-year-old Anna Payne, they headed south. It would take a week to journey to Montpelier, the Madison family estate in Orange County, Virginia.

Abigail Adams said that a chance to dine with Dolley Madison "is prized by all who are asked to her home."

After his marriage, Madison had kept workers busy adding to the family house.

Between 1797 and 1800, carpenters and bricklayers built a thirty-foot addition to the north end of the house. The Montpelier house had doubled in size. James's parents, James Sr. and Nelly, lived in the old half of the house. To enter one half of the house from the other, a person had to walk out one front door and then go in again through another. The new, two-story brick addition included a dining room, a sitting room, and bedrooms upstairs.

James Sr. was not in good health. He needed his oldest son James to help run the estate. The Madisons kept a telescope mounted on the front porch. A servant could watch the road in the distance and see when guests were coming. Dolley quickly learned the job of entertaining guests at Montpelier. Her niece, Mary Cutts, later wrote, "There are few houses in Virginia that gave a larger welcome."[18]

"There are few houses in Virginia that gave a larger welcome."

The Madisons dressed in black mourning clothes when they learned that Dolley's cousin, patriot Patrick Henry, had died on June 6, 1799. In December, more sad news reached Montpelier. George Washington had died of a throat infection. That year, James Madison returned to public service. He served as a member of the Virginia Assembly from Orange County. The Madisons stayed in the Virginia capital of Richmond during the assembly session between December 1799 and January 1800. Then, in February 1801, James

Madison Sr. died. He left Montpelier to James, along with about one hundred slaves.

The Election of 1800

In the presidential election of 1800, Federalist John Adams suffered defeat. He was not elected to serve a second term. By a twist of fate, Republican Thomas Jefferson and his running mate Aaron Burr both received 73 electoral ballots. The tie was finally broken by a vote in the House of Representatives. Thomas Jefferson was chosen to be the third President of the United States. Aaron Burr would be vice president.

On March 4, 1801, Jefferson asked James Madison to join his cabinet as secretary of state. Madison would be in charge of America's relations with all foreign countries. The death of James Sr. made it impossible for the Madisons to come to Washington right away. As they prepared for their journey, perhaps thirty-three-year-old Dolley Madison realized she would soon be thrust into the center of national politics.

The President's Hostess

The Madisons' carriage bounced ninety miles over rough dirt roads. It took five days to travel from Montpelier. On May 1, 1801, James, Dolley, Anna Payne, and young Payne Todd reached Washington, D.C.

A New Capital

No more than five thousand people lived in Washington, D.C. when it became the national capital in 1800. At one end of Pennsylvania Avenue stood the President's House. At the other end of the street stood the grand Capitol building. There was not much in between. In many parts of the city, woods still stood where streets were planned. The dirt roads were full of tree stumps. In rainy weather, they became great lakes of mud.

"Washington would be a beautiful city if it were built," commented one English visitor, "but as it is not, I cannot say much about it."[1] Politician Gouverneur Morris remarked, "We want nothing here but houses, cellars, kitchens . . . and other little [things] of this kind to make our city perfect." Morris also boasted that Washington was "the best city in the world for a future residence."[2]

Finding a Home

President Thomas Jefferson lived alone with his private secretary, Meriwether Lewis, at the President's House. The Madisons accepted Jefferson's invitation to stay with him until they could find a home of their own. The Madisons soon rented a new three-story house on Pennsylvania Avenue. It stood just four blocks from the President's House. It was one of a group of government houses called "the Six Buildings."

The Madisons returned to Montpelier for the summer. Before leaving, James Madison asked Dr. William Thornton to find a better home for his family to rent. Dr. Thornton was the architect who had designed the Capitol building. Thornton rented a house for the Madisons, 1333 F Street, right next door to his

The Nation's Capital

The decision to build the United States capital on the Potomac River was made at a private meeting. The meeting was hosted by then Secretary of State Thomas Jefferson on June 20, 1790, in Philadelphia. Jefferson's guests were Congress member James Madison and Secretary of the Treasury Alexander Hamilton. Jefferson and Madison controlled the Republican political party. They agreed to support Hamilton's plan for a national banking system. In exchange, Hamilton, as leader of the Federalist party, agreed to support something Jefferson and Madison wanted. They wanted the permanent national capital to be located on the Potomac River between Virginia and Maryland. Having the capital in the South would be good for the local economy. The bargain made by the three men that night made it possible for Washington, D.C. to be built.

William Birch painted this watercolor of the United States Capitol in about 1800. Only five thousand people lived in Washington, D.C. when it became the nation's capital in 1800.

own home. It was large and comfortable. The landlord promised to build a stable and carriage house for the Madison family, too. This would be their home while James Madison served as secretary of state.

The President's Hostess

Soon after she arrived in Washington, Dolley learned that President Jefferson needed her help. On May 27, 1801, a messenger knocked at the Madisons' door. He presented Dolley with a note: "Thomas Jefferson begs that either Mrs. Madison or Miss Payne will be so good as to dine with him today, to take care of his female friends expected."[3] Jefferson wanted Dolley to act as his hostess at a dinner party. Thomas Jefferson's wife Martha had died in 1782. He was a widower. His two married daughters, Martha and Mary, lived too far away to help him. Vice President Aaron Burr was also a widower. As the wife of Jefferson's chief cabinet member, Dolley was chosen.

> "Thomas Jefferson begs that either Mrs. Madison or Miss Payne will be so good as to dine with him today, to take care of his female friends expected."

Dolley proved a success at Jefferson's dinner that evening. After that, Jefferson often called on Dolley to serve as his hostess. Dinner was usually at three or four o'clock in the afternoon in those days. Congress member Manasseh Cutler described one meal. "Dined at the presidents," he wrote, " . . . Rice soup, round of beef, turkey, mutton, ham, . . . veal, . . . fried eggs, fried beef, a pie called macaroni which appeared to be a rich crust filled with . . . onions."[4]

The Social Whirl

The Madisons had become leading members of capital society. Massachusetts Senator John Quincy Adams remarked that Dolley had made her home "one of the social centers of the city."[5] Dolley became a leader of fashion, too. She was not afraid to dress in new styles of clothes, hats, and shoes. Before long, other women followed her example. "I care not for newness for its own sake," she told her sister Anna. "I take and use only that which is pleasing to me."[6]

Dolley made new friends in Washington. Among the closest were Hannah Nicholson Gallatin, the wife of Secretary of the Treasury Albert Gallatin. Another was Margaret Bayard Smith, whose husband, Samuel Harrison Smith, was the editor of *The Daily National Intelligencer*. It was Washington's first newspaper. Margaret Bayard Smith declared of Dolley, "Her manners are just what they ought to be. . . . She is really a lovely woman."[7]

Dolley enjoyed visiting people and making new friends. Her dark-green carriage soon became a common sight traveling along the city streets. Dolley seemed to fill her role in Washington society perfectly. As a Quaker farm girl, Dolley had learned that hard work and good habits won respect. While in Philadelphia, as a congress member's wife, she had quickly learned how to behave

Dolley Madison brought new styles of clothing to Washington. Many women began to follow her lead. This painting shows her in one of the Parisian gowns and elaborate turbans that became her trademarks.

among politicians. At Montpelier, she had become skilled in the art of entertaining large groups of people. A relative wrote that Dolley had "a desire to please, and a willingness to be pleased, which made her popular."[8]

Parties and Dinners

Thomas Jefferson was a shy man. He only opened the President's House to the public two times a year, on New Year's Day and the Fourth of July. But Dolley Madison eagerly opened her house on F Street to visitors. John Quincy Adams remarked, "On the first New Year's Day after she came . . . the custom was established of going from the White House to call on Mrs. Madison."[9]

President Jefferson usually held small dinners at the President's House. His guests were men who sat together and chatted about politics. The Madisons' dinner parties, however, were quite different. At one Madison dinner, John Quincy Adams found himself seated with "a company of about seventy persons of both sexes."[10] Dolley knew how to keep everyone in good spirits. One guest remembered, "Mrs. Madison . . . always finds time . . . to speak to everybody, [and she] never forgets the name of any one to whom she has been introduced . . . "[11] In fact, Dolley would become famous for her perfect memory.

Lewis and Clark

In 1800, France took control of the Louisiana Territory from the Spanish. The huge region stretched from the

Learning French

Marie-Angelique Turreau, the wife of the French ambassador, became one of Dolley's good friends. The two women often went walking and riding together. When together in private, Dolley said, "I crack my sides a laughing." Dolley explained that Marie-Angelique spoke "no English but we understand each other well."[12] In time, Marie-Angelique Turreau taught Dolley how to speak French. This was the language commonly spoken by diplomats at the time. Learning French helped contribute to the impression of Dolley as an accomplished lady.

Gulf of Mexico to Canada. In the spring of 1803, French First Consul Napoleon Bonaparte offered to sell the entire region to the United States for $15 million. After negotiations, when the treaty was finally signed in France, the United States doubled in size. The Louisiana Purchase included all of present-day Arkansas, Iowa, Missouri, and Nebraska, as well as parts of Louisiana, Minnesota, Oklahoma, Kansas, Colorado, Wyoming, Montana, North Dakota, and South Dakota.

In 1803, President Jefferson chose Meriwether Lewis and William Clark to explore the new territory. They would also try to find an inland water route to the Pacific Ocean. Congress agreed to spend $2,500 for their journey. Dolley and her many friends helped raise some additional money for equipment. Dolley knew Meriwether Lewis well. After all, he had been President Jefferson's private secretary. When Lewis and Clark successfully returned in 1806, they gratefully gave Dolley some of the silver knives, forks, and spoons they had used for cooking.

The Merry Affair

In November 1803, a new British ambassador, Anthony Merry, and his wife Elizabeth, arrived in the United States. After reaching Washington, D.C., Ambassador Merry made his first visit to the President's House.

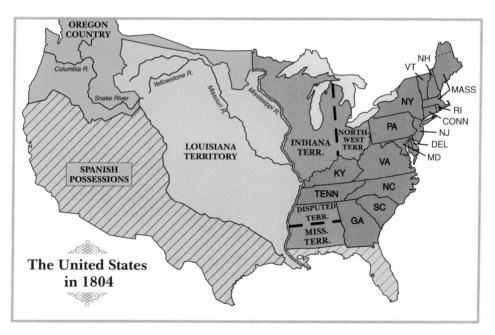

The Louisiana Purchase nearly doubled the size of the United States. This is a map of the United States in 1804 showing the Louisiana Territory.

The ambassador dressed in his best clothes. A handsome sword dangled at his side. Merry was greatly surprised when President Jefferson greeted him in everyday clothes. Jefferson even wore old slippers on his feet. This was Jefferson's democratic style. He insisted on greeting the British ambassador the same way he would greet a common worker. The shocked ambassador had expected to be treated with much greater respect.

Three days later, at a dinner at the President's House, the Merrys felt insulted again. When dinner was announced, Jefferson turned to his hostess, Dolley Madison. He held out his arm, and began to escort her to the table. The normal social custom required that Jefferson take the arm of the lady of honor, Mrs. Merry. But Jefferson wanted to show that in a democracy no one got special attention. Dolley hurriedly whispered, "Take Mrs. Merry," but Jefferson ignored her. The other guests were stunned by his rude behavior. The wife of the Spanish ambassador later declared to Dolley, "This will be the cause of war!"[13]

Secretary of State Madison finally took Mrs. Merry's arm. He led her to the table. The ambassador was forced to find a seat for himself. Merry finally found a seat at the far end of the table.

Dinner at the Madisons' House

A few days later at the Madisons' house on F Street, the Merrys were insulted again. Perhaps Secretary of State Madison was following instructions from the president. When the dinner was announced, Madison escorted

Hannah Nicholson Gallatin instead of Elizabeth Merry. Ambassador Merry walked his wife in to dinner. When the Merrys reached the table, they discovered Hannah Gallatin sitting in the place of honor. Stubbornly, Elizabeth Merry waited until Mrs. Gallatin finally offered her the chair.

Mrs. Merry then made a comment about Dolley Madison's meal. The food had been prepared using simple Virginian recipes. There were no fancy European foods. Mrs. Merry remarked that it was "more like a harvest home supper than the entertainment of a

Ice Cream

On February 10, 1802, Senator Samuel Mitchill penned a letter to his wife. In it, he described a delicious dessert he had eaten at the President's House. "Among other things ice-creams were produced," he wrote, " . . . in covers of warm pastry . . . " The ice cream, together with the flaky dough, made a tasty combination, "as if the ice had just been taken from the oven," Mitchill declared.[14] According to legend, it was Dolley Madison who first served ice cream at the White House. She did enjoy ice cream and served it often. In truth, though, the dessert was already popular by the time Dolley reached Washington, D.C.[15]

Secretary of State."[16] Dolley calmly replied that she thought a lot of good food was better than a little fancy food.

The American treatment of the British Merrys had hurt foreign relations. To insult a foreign ambassador was the same as insulting a foreign country itself. In the days that followed, Dolley tried to smooth things over. Once, she heard that Elizabeth Merry was trying to find a certain perfume. Dolley sent her a bottle of her own rose-scented perfume. In time, the two women became good friends.

A Sad Knee

Dolley developed an open sore on her knee in June 1805. The sore refused to heal. In a letter to her sister Anna, Dolley explained how she had been in bed "for ten days with a sad knee."[17] Much of the time, James remained at her side, talking and reading to her. He was always ready to help if needed. Dolley's knee did not get better, however.

At the end of July, Dolley and James traveled to Philadelphia. They rented a room and had Dr. Philip Syng Physick come to see her. Dr. Physick was one of America's leading doctors. He examined the leg and put a long wooden splint wrapped with cloth on it. The splint was so tight that Dolley could not even sit up. She reported to Anna, "Dr. Physick has seen my knee and says he will cure it in a month."[18] James stayed with her for as long as possible. On October 23, he finally had to return to his duties in Washington.

A letter from Dolley Madison to her sister, Anna Cutts, dated August 19, 1805. At this time, Dolley developed a sore on her knee, which she called, in her letter to Anna, a "sad knee."

During the next three weeks, the Madisons lived apart. It was their first separation, since their marriage. It took about four days for a letter to travel between Washington and Philadelphia. The Madisons wrote to one another constantly. "Think of thy wife! who thinks and dreams of thee!" Dolley wrote in one letter. She also advised James, who worked constantly, to "take as much relaxation, & pleasure as you can."[19]

> "My beloved, our hearts understand each other."

As her knee slowly healed she happily declared, "I am getting well as fast as I can."[20] Forced to stay in bed, unable to move her leg, Dolley greatly missed her husband. On October 25, she penned, "My beloved, our hearts understand each other."[21] Finally, at the end of November, Dolley's knee was better. Happily, James Madison and her sister Anna came to bring her home.

Family Changes

In March 1804, Dolley's twenty-five-year-old sister Anna Payne married Massachusetts congress member Richard Cutts. (The part of Massachusetts Cutts represented would become the state of Maine in 1820.) Anna had lived with Dolley since childhood. Dolley treated her as much like a daughter as a sister. She would miss her company very much.

Dolley suffered even greater sadness. In October 1807, her mother Mary Payne died, probably of a stroke. A few months later, her sister Mary died of the lung disease tuberculosis. To her old friend, Eliza Collins, Dolley revealed her feelings: "When I trace the sad events that have occurred to me, I feel as if I should die [too]."[22]

The Election of 1808

During 1808, it became clear that Thomas Jefferson, after serving two terms as president, planned to retire. Republicans wanted James Madison to take his place in the President's House. For a time, Vice President George Clinton also campaigned for the nomination. New York Senator Samuel Mitchill remarked, "The Secretary of State has a wife to aid [him]. The Vice-President has [no] female [help] on his side. And in these two respects Mr. Madison is going greatly ahead of him."[23] Dolley's influence and charm were a great aid to her husband. In the end, the Republicans nominated James Madison as their candidate. The Federalists chose Charles C. Pinckney of South Carolina to run against him.

James Madison refused to campaign. Back then, it was considered bad manners for a presidential candidate to make speeches and spend time shaking hands. At the house on F Street, Dolley did much of the campaigning for him. She gladly gave dinners and parties for congress members, to win their support. Margaret Bayard Smith declared, "Mrs. Madison . . . sometimes even [changed] political enemies into personal friends."[24] "Politics is the business of men," Dolley once declared. "I don't care what offices they may hold. . . . I care only about people."[25]

The Madisons prepared to leave Washington for their summer vacation at Montpelier in 1808. Before they left, on July 4, Dolley reviewed a cavalry troop that passed before the Madison house. She presented them with a beautiful flag and gave a patriotic speech. Once at home in Orange, Virginia, Dolley continued campaigning for her husband.

> **"I was beaten by Mr. and Mrs. Madison,"** he said. **"I might have had a better chance had I faced Mr. Madison alone."**
>
> —Charles C. Pinckney

In the fall, citizens in the seventeen states cast their votes and chose electors. The electors represented them in making a final vote on December 7 in the House of Representatives. The final vote revealed: Madison 122, Pinckney 47, and Clinton 6. James Madison had been elected fourth President of the United States. Pinckney admitted Dolley's important role in the election. "I was beaten by Mr. and Mrs. Madison," he said. "I might have had a better chance had I faced Mr. Madison alone."[26]

Queen Dolley

At dawn on March 4, 1809, cannons boomed at Washington's navy yard and at nearby Fort Warburton. As the sun rose, local military companies gathered for escort duty. On the roads, visitors from all over the country crowded into the city. People came to Washington to celebrate the inauguration of James Madison as fourth president of the United States.

A New President

The Madisons traveled from the house on F Street by carriage. Military horsemen rode beside them. Slowly down Pennsylvania Avenue, they passed the thousands who lined the street. At the Capitol, an even greater crowd waited to greet them.

Army and navy bands filled the air with the music of drums and trumpets. James Madison walked up the Capitol steps. The inauguration took place in the House of Representatives. First, Madison gave his inaugural address. Margaret Bayard Smith noticed that "Mr. Madison was extremely pale and trembled . . . when he first began to speak, but soon gained confidence . . . "[1] After his ten-minute speech, Madison took the oath of office. He was sworn in by Supreme Court Chief Justice John Marshall.

Afterwards, back at the house on F Street, the Madisons welcomed visitors. Margaret Bayard Smith recalled, "The street was full of carriages and people . . . the house was completely filled. . . . Near the door of the drawing room Mr. and Mrs. Madison stood to receive their company. She looked extremely beautiful."[2]

The Inaugural Ball

Each of the first three presidents had ended his first day in office by going to bed early. But the Madisons had agreed to do things differently this time. An inaugural ball for four hundred invited guests was held at Long's Hotel on Capitol Hill. Since that night, every president

James Madison was inaugurated as the fourth president of the United States on March 4, 1809. This illustration shows the Capitol and Pennsylvania Avenue around the time of his inauguration.

of the United States has ended his inauguration day with a ball like the Madisons'.

The ball started at seven o'clock, when the band played "Jefferson's March." "Am I too early?" Thomas Jefferson asked as he entered. "You must tell me how to behave, for it is more than forty years since I have been to a ball."[3] Next the band played "Madison's March." The new president entered the hall, along with Dolley and Anna Cutts. Dolley wore a pale yellow velvet dress with a very long skirt. On her head was a French turban of the same yellow velvet and white satin. The turban had two bird of paradise feathers on it. A pearl necklace hung around Dolley's neck. She wore earrings and bracelets, too. Altogether, her outfit was quite remarkable. Margaret Bayard Smith declared that "she looked and moved like a queen."[4] Another guest commented, "Mrs. Madison is a handsome woman—looks much younger than her husband. . . . It is impossible . . . to be with her and not be pleased. There is something very fascinating about her."[5]

At the ball, James Madison seemed completely tired. Soon after dinner, he excused himself. He and Dolley went home. The other guests, however, danced until the band stopped playing at midnight.

Decorating the White House

Dolley had become the "Lady Presidentess."[6] As the new president's wife, it was her job to decorate the President's House. The house had become very rundown and needed improvements. Congress members appropriated $20,000 for repairs and new furniture. Dolley called on the help of architect Benjamin H. Latrobe to decorate.

Dolley's Turbans

Dolley did not invent the turban style of hat, but she made them very popular in the United States. Dolley designed and made turbans for her sisters and her friends. Turbans made her look taller and helped her stand out in a crowd.

Dolley Madison helped make the turban style of hat popular in the United States. At her husband's first inaugural ball, she wore a turban with two feathers in it. This painting of Dolley wearing a turban was done much later in her life.

Already the President's House was being called the "White House" by many people. It was still an unfinished building. Stacks of lumber and piles of stone cluttered the yard. While president, Thomas Jefferson had filled the White House with furniture from his Virginia home, Monticello. Jefferson took the furniture with him when he left office. Dolley and James moved into empty rooms.

Mrs. Madison's Sitting Room

Dolley and Latrobe began by decorating two rooms. The small parlor or sitting room is called the Red Room today. The large oval drawing room is now known as the Blue Room. Just six days after Madison's inauguration, Latrobe spent $3,150 buying eight large mirrors.

Dolley and Latrobe wished to create an American house for the president. All of the furniture Dolley chose for the White House was made by American craftspeople. Dolley bought candlesticks and lamps of the newest design. There were no electric lights in those days. Most Americans burned tallow candles. Made from animal fat, tallow candles sputtered and smelled. Instead, Dolley bought expensive spermaceti wax candles made from whale blubber. These candles gave off a soft, even glow.

Latrobe searched Philadelphia, New York, and Baltimore for the furniture they needed. He bought a new carpet, some side tables and card tables, a piano that cost $450, a guitar, and even a chess set. The chair seats and sofa coverings for the sitting room were a bright yellow color.

The Oval Drawing Room

For the large Oval Drawing Room, Latrobe bought a Brussels carpet. The Finlays of Baltimore made thirty-six gilded cane-seat chairs. Two sofas and four large cushioned chairs were also bought at a total cost of $1,111.

Dolley desired red silk curtains for the room. Latrobe could not find enough red silk in either New York or Philadelphia. "I am therefore forced to give you crimson Velvet curtains," he wrote to Dolley.[7] She loved the color crimson, which was a deep, dark red. Latrobe worried that the crimson velvet would be too heavy and bright for the room. "The curtains! Oh the terrible velvet curtains!" he exclaimed after he saw the cloth.[8]

The empty Oval Drawing Room was where Abigail Adams had hung her laundry to dry. Dolley and Latrobe made it into one of the most beautiful public rooms ever seen in the United States. Altogether, Dolley and Latrobe spent $12,669.31 decorating the two rooms, including the wallpapering and painting. The improvements helped the White House become America's proper national home. "The President's house is a perfect palace," one of Dolley's visitors later declared.[9]

Open House

Dolley held her first weekly drawing room party in March 1809. No written invitations were sent and anyone could visit. Dolley personally greeted and spoke to everyone who came through the door. She treated every guest as if he or she were a dear friend.

Catharine Akerly Mitchill remembered going to one open house. The excitement began before she even arrived. She saw as she neared the White House, "the great number of Carriages, all drawn . . . towards the great center of attraction." As the Mitchill carriage reached the front door, she heard, "the sound of sweet music." Soon, she found herself among "almost every important person in Washington . . . both male and female."[10]

When writer Washington Irving arrived on a visit in January 1811, he was surprised. He stepped from "a dirty stage coach and muddy roads [into the beauty] of Mrs. Madison's drawing room. . . . Here I was most [nicely] received; found a crowded collection of great and little men, of ugly old women and beautiful young ones."[11] Irving described Dolley as a fine lady "who has a smile and a pleasant word for everybody."[12]

> "Here I was most [nicely] received; found a crowded collection of great and little men, of ugly old women and beautiful young ones."

Dolley's parties established the White House as the social center of Washington. She held regular gatherings on Wednesday nights that brought together Republicans and Federalists, cabinet members and congress members, men and women. During these evenings, guests stood in groups. People moved from

Dolley Madison was the first person to decorate the Yellow Oval Room in 1809. Upstairs from the Oval Drawing Room, or Blue Room, this room would be used in different ways by many presidents and first ladies. First Lady Michelle Obama hosts Jordan's Queen Rania in the Yellow Oval Room on April 23, 2009.

group to group and took part in different conversations. Dolley made a great effort to make sure everyone remained friendly. Political enemies often found they could talk together and work out differences in this pleasant atmosphere. Servants carried large trays around the room. They served food and drinks to the guests. One visitor recalled, "Tea and coffee and afterwards cold punch with glasses of [wine] and cakes are handed round. . . ."[13]

First Impressions

Young William Campbell Preston felt awkward during his first evening visit to the White House. He stood next to President Madison without saying a word. Then, Dolley entered the room. Instead of greeting other guests, she walked right up to the young man. She asked, "Are you William Campbell Preston, son of my old friend . . . Sally Campbell?" He said that he was. "Sit down my son," she warmly told him, "for you are my son, and I am the first person who ever saw you in this world."[14] Dolley introduced the surprised young man to the president who then shook his hand. By paying such close attention to the young stranger, Dolley had made a friend for life. Young Elbridge Gerry Jr. felt much the same way when he met Dolley. "She treated me more like a son than a stranger," he said.[15]

> "She moves like a goddess, and she looks a queen."

At her parties, Dolley walked about making sure everyone was comfortable. Catharine Mitchill stated, "I never saw a lady who enjoyed society more than she does."[16] The Danish ambassador was also impressed. "I never have seen any duchess, princess or queen," he declared, "whose manners, with equal dignity, blended equal sweetness." He added, "She moves like a goddess, and she looks a queen."[17]

Not everyone loved Dolley. Rosalie Stier Calvert mockingly referred to her as "Queen Dolla lolla."[18] Some of Dolley's habits were considered bad manners by certain people. Dolley took snuff (powdered tobacco) up her nose. This was a habit thought by many as crude and old-fashioned. Dolley also often embraced people when she met them. She was always glad to give a kiss in greeting, too. In those days, most women wore no make up. It is believed by some that Dolley wore red lipstick and also rubbed red rouge on her cheeks to give them color.

The hostess with the warm smile, flowing clothes, and waving ostrich feathers on her hat was not at all like her husband. At a social event at the White House, one guest saw that James Madison "was pushed and jostled about like a common citizen—but not her ladyship."[19] While James often seemed pale and tired, Dolley showed only health and energy.

As the leader of Washington society, Dolley had become a national figure. In those days it was unusual for a woman's name to appear in print. Yet Dolley had her picture on the cover of a popular Philadelphia magazine. Common citizens often showed up at the White House door to meet her. The United States was still a young, new country. George Washington had been the first person to symbolize the nation. Now it seemed Dolley was taking her place as one of the most famous and loved people in the United States.

Inside the White House

For the first time, the White House had become a real home. Dolley and James always had family members around them. Payne Todd lived with them, when he was not at school in Baltimore. The household also included Anna and Richard Cutts and their children, whenever they were in the city. Dolley's sister Lucy and her sons often visited. Dolley's cousin, Edward Coles, served as

A Conversation Starter

William C. Preston once noticed that Dolley entered a drawing room party with a book in her hand. When she remarked that the demands of society used up much of her time, Preston replied: "Still you have time to read." "Oh, no;" she replied, "Not a word; I have this book in my hand—a very fine copy of Don Quixote—to have something not ungraceful to say, and if need be to supply a word of talk."[20] If she had nothing else for conversation, Dolley could always talk about the book she carried.

President Madison's personal secretary. He lived there, also. Dolley owned a pet, a brightly feathered macaw named Polly. Talking in its cage, Polly seemed like part of the family, too.

Doorkeeper John Sioussat helped Dolley run the White House. Maids and servants followed his orders. French chef Pierre Roux prepared delicious meals with excellent French wines. Dolley held more formal dinners than any president's wife before or after her. The Madisons' official dinners took place once a week. As many as thirty guests attended. At a Madison dinner a slave or servant stood behind each guest. They made sure that all went well. Dolley increased the number of presidential servants from fourteen to thirty. At James's suggestion, Dolley still always sat at the head of the table. James often fell silent in large groups. Dolley, however, enjoyed leading conversations. She spoke her mind and persuaded guests to accept her husband's political views. Dolley could discuss any subject likely to come up. One guest commented, "She talks a great deal and in such quick, beautiful tones."[21]

At her dinners, Dolley usually served American foods. She searched for special recipes from friends all across the country. It is believed she offered her own recipes in exchange, including her method for making ice cream. Women were honored and pleased to think their recipes were being served at the White House. The good food at Dolley's table, the lovely setting, the comfortable furniture, and fine atmosphere made guests feel relaxed and happy.

Washington Ladies

Whenever James Madison held his cabinet meetings, Dolley hosted meetings with the cabinet wives. The cabinet wives talked about current events. Dolley also attended debates in Congress and Supreme Court trials. She encouraged other women to join her. Before this time, ladies were not often seen in those places.

When Dolley and her many friends sat in the audience,

John Payne Todd, Dolley's son from her first marriage, stayed at the White House when he was not in school in Baltimore, Maryland.

Preventing a Duel

In 1811, Virginia congress member John Randolph publicly insulted fellow member John Eppes. Eppes was Thomas Jefferson's son-in-law. Louis Serurier, the French ambassador noted, "These gentlemen will fight a duel . . . next Monday and often what usually happens in these duels in America one can expect one of the two men will remain dead."[22] In this case, no pistols were ever fired, however. Dolley Madison prevented the duel. Somehow, Dolley even got Randolph to apologize to Eppes. "Everybody is astonished," exclaimed Serurier, " . . . and all the credit of the affair [is] Mrs. Madison's. Nobody knows what she said, but everybody can know what she accomplished."[23]

politicians often behaved differently. During one trial at the Supreme Court, Attorney General William Pinkney had just finished speaking. He was sitting down, when Dolley and several other ladies entered. Pinkney immediately stood and gave his speech again. This time, however, he used fewer arguments and chose his words more carefully. He did not want to use rough language in a lady's presence. It seemed that wherever Dolley went she made an impact.

Chapter

6

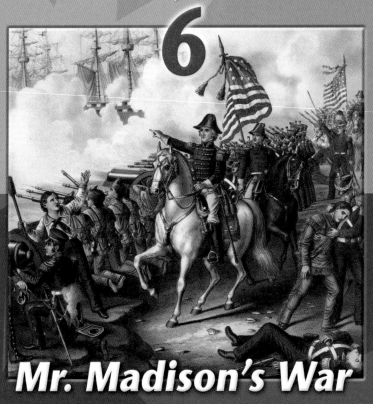

Mr. Madison's War

"I believe there will be war, as Mr. Madison sees no end to our [problems] without it," Dolley wrote to Anna Cutts in December 1811.[1] For years, relations between the United States and Great Britain had not been good. Great Britain and France were at war. As a result, Great Britain tried to keep United States merchants from trading with France. To add sailors to its navy, British warships sometimes stopped American merchant ships at sea. At gun point, the British forced American sailors to join the British Navy. This form of kidnapping was called impressment.

The War Hawks

Many American congress members were outraged by these British acts. A group of fierce new congress members took the nickname War Hawks. They included Henry Clay of Kentucky, John C. Calhoun of South Carolina, and Felix Grundy of Tennessee. These angry politicians openly called for war with Great Britain. Dolley became friends with many of these young congress members. Henry Clay thought Dolley was "the most charming of ladies it has ever been my good fortune to encounter."[2]

By the spring of 1812, relations with Great Britain had grown worse. The British Navy continued to seize American ships and carry off sailors from their crews. Finally, on June 1, 1812, President Madison sent a message to the House of Representatives. To Congress, he listed "the . . . injuries and [insults] which have been heaped on our country."[3] In the days that followed, the House of Representatives and the Senate both voted for war. On June 18, President Madison signed an official declaration of war. This began the War of 1812.

Early Fights

Federalists in the New England states were not in favor of the war. They called it "Mr. Madison's War." The supporters of the war called it "The Second War of

A White House Wedding

In March of 1812, Dolley wrote to her sister Anna Cutts: "Before this reaches you Lucy will be married to Judge Todd of Kentucky! Yes, sudden as it is, we must be reconciled to it from her choice of a Man of the most estimable character, best principles, & high talents."[4] Associate Supreme Court Justice Thomas Todd had been courting Lucy Payne Washington for some time. She had been a widow since the death of her first husband, George Steptoe Washington. On March 29, President Madison gave the bride away. It was the first wedding ever held in the White House.

American Independence." Some of the first fighting took place along the United States' border with Canada, which was British territory. In the summer of 1812, British General Isaac Brock boldly crossed his small army into Michigan. In a panic, on August 16, General William Hull surrendered Fort Detroit and his entire American army without firing a single shot. When they learned the terrible news, both James and Dolley Madison were shocked.

Surprisingly, America's first victories in the war were battles at sea. At the time, there were no more than seventeen warships in the U.S. Navy. Great Britain had a huge navy of about seven hundred warships.

The British Navy also had more experienced sailors. However, on August 19, 1812, the United States warship *Constitution*, commanded by Captain Isaac Hull, defeated the British warship *Guerriere*. During the fight, one of the *Constitution*'s sailors saw a cannonball bounce off her hull. "Huzza," he shouted, "her sides are made of iron."[5] In the United States, the story of "Old Ironsides" was celebrated everywhere. The *Constitution*'s thrilling victory was soon followed by others.

Captured Flags

Dolley gave more parties during the war than she ever had before. As many as five hundred guests "squeezed" into one of her Wednesday night drawing room parties. Dolley's parties showed the country that even in wartime, society could go on as normal.

After the American Navy defeated the British ships *Guerriere* and *Macedonian* in 1812, Navy officers presented Dolley with flags taken from the ships. The captured flags of the *Macedonian* were presented to Dolley by a navy lieutenant at a White House party. "Cheers of welcome were [shouted]," recalled Senator Samuel Mitchill, "'Yankee Doodle' was played, the [flags] were [shown], and finally laid on the floor at the feet of Mrs. Madison."[6]

The Election of 1812

Dolley Madison had made a great impression during her husband's four-year term in office. Kentucky senator John Pope joked that Dolley made "a very good

The battle between the United States warship Constitution *and the British warship* Guerriere *on August 19, 1812, is shown in this 1813 painting by Thomas Birch. Because of this battle, the* Constitution *received its nickname "Old Ironsides."*

president and must not be turned out."[7] As the election of 1812 neared, Dolley again campaigned for her husband with all of her social skills.

But not all Republicans favored Madison. New York Republicans called upon New York City Mayor DeWitt Clinton to run for president. The Federalists could not settle on a candidate of their own. They decided to support Clinton, too.

The success of the American navy boosted hopes that the United States could win the war. Western settlers wanted the war to continue. They demanded revenge for the loss of Fort Detroit. Many voters in the northeastern states no longer supported the president. The war was hurting ship owners and sailors who depended on fishing and trade to earn their livings. At last, the electors of the eighteen states cast their ballots. Louisiana had become the newest state in 1812. Madison learned that he and his war still had the support of the people. The vote revealed: Madison 128, Clinton 89. James Madison had won a second term as president.

The War Spirit

Dolley watched her husband take his second oath as president on the sunny day of March 4, 1813. The United States had been at war for more than a year. Dolley did her best to give the country hope. She made sure that life in Washington went on as usual. She reviewed parading troops like a general. Soldiers often marched by the White House. Many times, she invited them inside and served them food and drink. Madison's servant, Paul Jennings, said, "She was beloved by every body in Washington."[8]

Along the border with Canada, the war continued. On September 10, 1813, American Captain Oliver H. Perry commanded a small fleet of warships on Lake Erie. Aboard the *Niagara*, Perry sailed through the middle of a strong British squadron of ships. The *Niagara*'s cannons roared, smashing five of the enemy ships with cannonballs. After winning the Battle of Lake Erie, Perry could proudly report, "We have met the enemy and they are ours."[9]

Perry's exciting victory won the American forces total control of Lake Erie. Within days, American General William Henry Harrison recaptured Fort Detroit. Pushing ahead, Harrison's army attacked a force of British soldiers and their American Indian allies at the Thames River. The Americans won a stunning victory at the Battle of the Thames in October 1813. In that fight, the great Shawnee leader and British ally Tecumseh was killed.

Secretary and Nurse

In the late spring of 1813, Edward Coles fell ill. He was Dolley's cousin and President Madison's private secretary. Coles went to Philadelphia for treatment. While he was away, Dolley took over his work. She served as her husband's secretary. Madison dictated letters to her. He discussed all of his presidential business with her.

Oliver H. Perry (standing) in a small boat heading for the Niagara *warship during the Battle of Lake Erie on September 10, 1813. Perry's victory in this battle gave the American forces control of Lake Erie.*

Before Coles returned to his duties, President Madison fell sick with a fever in June 1813. For a while, his life was in great danger. Dolley nursed him day and night, almost never leaving his side. On July 29, an exhausted Dolley wrote to Hannah Gallatin, "You have [heard] no doubt, of the illness of my Husband. . . . I attended his bed for nearly five weeks! Even now, I watch over him, as I would an infant."[10] Completely tired, she wrote to Edward Coles. "It is three weeks now [that] I have nursed him. . . . But now that I see he will get well I feel as if I might die myself from fatigue. . . ."[11]

A British Invasion

In 1813, British warships began months of raiding along America's Atlantic coast. In early August 1814, Dolley angrily wrote to her son Payne that "the British on our shores are stealing & destroying private property."[12] Finally, on August 19, four thousand British troops landed at Benedict, Maryland. The enemy was just forty-five miles north of Washington, D.C.

British Admiral George Cockburn boasted that Dolley Madison had better run away from the White House. He sent word that "Unless she left, the house would be burned over her head."[13] He threatened to capture Dolley and march her as a prisoner through the streets of London, England. Secretary of War John Armstrong could not believe that Washington would be the British target.

Valuable Documents

The threat of British attack brought action at the State Department. Chief Clerk John Graham and two other workers, Stephen Pleasanton and Josiah King, made plans. They would save the U.S. government's most valuable papers. Into cloth bags carefully went the original Declaration of Independence, the Articles of Confederation, the Constitution, George Washington's Revolutionary War commission as Commander-in-chief of the army, and many other valuable papers. When the British landed in Maryland, Pleasanton loaded wagons and carried off the priceless documents. In Leesburg, Virginia, he safely hid them in an empty stone house.

Panic in Washington

On August 23, James Madison left Washington to visit the American army camp in Maryland. He spent the morning with the soldiers and found them healthy and in good spirits. Madison returned home at dark to spend a few hours with his wife. It would be their last night in the White House.

On August 24, Madison hugged Dolley and kissed her goodbye. He told her that he and his officers would be back in time for dinner. Then he mounted his horse and headed again to the army camps at Bladensburg, Maryland.

Dolley spent much of the morning at an upstairs window with a telescope, waiting for her husband. Most of the city had left. The mayor of Washington, Dr. James Blake, came twice and begged her to leave, too.

Dolley waited all that long afternoon. When James Smith rode to the White House shouting, "'Clear out, clear out!" she knew it was time to go. Two New Yorkers, Jacob Barker and Robert G. L. DePeyster, helped her save the painting of George Washington. Barker, a ship owner, was very impressed with Dolley's bravery that day. He later named one of his merchant ships the *Lady Madison*.

The Escape

At last, Dolley hurried out the White House front door. She climbed inside a waiting carriage. Already inside were Charles Carroll, Anna Cutts, Richard Cutts, and Dolley's maid, Sukey. They left the city only a couple of hours before the enemy arrived.

The Madisons' coachman, Joe Bolen, whipped up the horses. The carriage rushed west to Georgetown, Maryland. A witness soon saw "Mrs. Madison in her carriage flying full speed through Georgetown, accompanied by an officer carrying a drawn sword."[14] They rested a short time at Secretary of the Navy William Jones's house. Then the carriage continued to Charles Carroll's home, Belle Vue.

Surprisingly, Dolley then insisted that the frightened coachman drive back toward the White House. She still hoped to find her husband. Dolley and James did meet for a few minutes beside the Potomac River south of Washington. But President Madison could not stay with her. Duty demanded that he help reorganize the defeated American army. He and Dolley agreed to meet again soon in Great Falls, Virginia. That night, Dolley stayed at a friend's home in nearby Rokeby. From the open window, she shuddered to see red flames rising in the sky above Washington.

The Burning of Washington

At sundown, August 24, British sailors and marines marched into Washington. They were commanded by Admiral Cockburn and Major General Robert Ross. One year earlier, American soldiers had set fire to government buildings in York (present-day Toronto), Canada. The British wanted revenge. The troops marched to the capitol. British officers ordered furniture, doors, chairs, and desks thrown in a pile. The troops tossed burning torches onto it. Soon, flames poured out through broken windows.

Admiral Cockburn and Major General Ross next ordered the sailors and marines down Pennsylvania Avenue to the White House. It was growing dark when the troops arrived. Tired and hungry, they entered the deserted mansion. They were amazed to discover dinner on the table waiting for them. It was the untouched meal Dolley had prepared for her husband

The British army setting fire to the White House on August 24, 1814.

and his friends. British Captain Harry Smith exclaimed, "We found supper all ready . . . and . . . some very good wine also."[15]

Admiral Cockburn picked up an old hat of James Madison's and a cushion from one of Dolley's chairs. He would keep these as souvenirs. Then he ordered the mansion set on fire. At about midnight, the British invaders went from room to room with torches. They set fire to whatever would burn. All of Dolley's chairs, tables, and rugs, the piano, and even the guitar were piled up and lit.

Flames burst through the windows and licked up the outside of the house. In less than an hour, the wooden floors of the White House crashed in burning heaps. The British invaders moved next to burn the nearby Treasury building. Tongues of flame and clouds of sparks rose high into the Washington sky.

The Hurricane

The next morning, August 25, the British troops burned more government buildings. The British would have burned the Patent Office, but Dr. William Thornton stopped them at the door. He persuaded the enemy that the inventions inside were valuable to all people, not just Americans.

The burning of Washington ended early in the afternoon when a hurricane suddenly struck the city. A British soldier exclaimed that "roofs of houses were torn off and carried into the air like sheets of paper . . . " The wind roared and the rain poured down hard. "Many . . .

houses," the soldier continued, " . . . were blown down, and thirty of our men . . . were buried beneath their ruins."[16] The rains of the surprising storm put out much of the fire.

At last, the British decided to leave the city. In the evening, the enemy marched away into the darkness. They returned to their ships on the Patuxent River in Maryland.

A Ruined City

On August 25, Dolley Madison had arrived at Wiley's tavern in Great Falls, Virginia. It was the place where she had agreed to meet her husband. Dolley and her servant Sukey went upstairs to wait for him. "Mrs. Madison!" yelled the woman tavern keeper up the staircase. "If that's you, come down and go out! Your husband has got mine out fighting. . . . You shan't stay in my house; so get out!"[17] Only the start of the terrible storm convinced the angry woman to let Dolley stay and wait. James Madison never did arrive there.

It took another three days before Dolley found her way back to Washington. Dolley ordered her carriage to drive past the smoking remains of the White House. Margaret Bayard Smith saw that her friend "could scarcely speak without tears." Dolley later sadly said, "My whole heart mourned for my country!"[18] Lawyer William Wirt described the damage he saw. "I went to look at the ruins of the President's House," he declared. "The rooms [are now] nothing but unroofed naked walls, cracked . . . and blackened with fire."[19]

The ruins of the U.S. Capitol after the British invaded Washington, setting fire to many buildings. A hurricane helped put out the flames after the attack.

Crowds of people gathered to cheer Dolley's return to Washington. She smiled bravely and waved. "We shall rebuild Washington City," she told one woman. "The enemy cannot frighten a free people."[20] That same day, James Madison also safely returned to the city. Husband and wife were finally reunited.

The Octagon House

"I know not where we are [to live]," James Madison declared.[21] The burning of the White House left the Madisons homeless. French ambassador Louis Serurier quickly offered his house to the Madison family. On September 18, 1814, the Madisons moved into the Octagon House at the corner of New York Avenue and Eighteenth Street. The house did not, in fact, have the eight sides of an octagon. It had two rectangular wings and a round central tower.

At the three-story brick Octagon House, Dolley held a weekly drawing room party in the fall of 1814, just two days after the return of Congress. The Octagon House was not as grand as the White House. Dolley no longer had her fine lamps. At one party, she had servants stand all through the house holding torches to give light.

The Treaty of Ghent

In the hope of ending the war, President Madison had sent a peace commission to Europe. The American peace commissioners included John Quincy Adams, Albert Gallatin, Henry Clay, Jonathan Russell, and James Bayard. Dolley's twenty-one-year-old son Payne Todd traveled with the commission as a secretary. In the city of Ghent (in present-day Belgium), they met with members of a British commission. On December 24, 1814, these diplomats agreed upon a treaty ending the war.

America's greatest victory in the War of 1812 happened after the peace treaty at Ghent was arranged. On January 8, 1815, American General Andrew Jackson's army fought the enemy. About 2,600 British troops were killed, wounded, and captured at the Battle of New Orleans. Jackson's army suffered only seven dead and six wounded. News traveled slowly. It took three weeks for Dolley and all of Washington to learn of Jackson's stunning victory.

Ten days later, a coach pulled by four galloping horses rolled down Pennsylvania Avenue. At the

Octagon House, a messenger sprang from his seat. He carried a copy of the Treaty of Ghent. The news of the peace treaty greatly excited the Madisons. The cabinet joined President Madison to study the document upstairs. At the same time, Dolley opened the downstairs to the public. By early evening, her drawing room was filled with excited guests. "And what a happy scene it was!" described one reporter. Dolley moved among the crowd, exchanging congratulations. "No one could doubt, [who saw her smile] that all uncertainty was at an end," exclaimed a witness.[22]

After a careful reading, President Madison signed the treaty. More than two thousand American troops had died fighting in the war. And more than forty-five hundred had been wounded. The war had ended in a draw. No new territory had been won. No new promises between the two countries had been made. But it was certain that Great Britain would no longer impress American sailors. The War of 1812 had won the United States respect on land and sea. John Adams boldly declared that President Madison had "acquired more glory, and established more Union, than . . . Washington, Adams and Jefferson, put together."[23]

The National Capital

The war had filled Americans with a great sense of patriotism. The White House and the Capitol had become national symbols of the American government. The story of Dolley Madison saving the portrait of George Washington became a national legend.

General Andrew Jackson (on a white horse) leading his army during the Battle of New Orleans. This was the United States army's greatest victory during the War of 1812.

On October 17, 1814, Congress voted to keep the capital in Washington, D.C. The White House, the Capitol, and other government buildings would be repaired and rebuilt. The burning of the city left many poor citizens, especially servants, out of work. Many abandoned children needed help. In October 1815, Marcia Burnes Van Ness founded the Washington Female Orphan Asylum. It was a needed home for orphan girls. Dolley quickly joined as the "First Directress."[24] She paid for a milk cow and offered her skills with needle and thread. She gladly sewed clothes for the orphans.

Forty-seven-year-old Dolley, with her smile and cheerful conversation, was a welcome sight in the

The Octagon House in Washington, D.C. This is the house that Dolley and James Madison lived in after the British destroyed the White House.

battered city. She gave Washington citizens faith in the future. It seemed to many that Dolley Madison had become the most popular person in the United States. Soldiers, marching home from the war, stopped at the Octagon House to cheer her. "Everybody loves Mrs. Madison," Henry Clay once remarked in front of Dolley. She immediately replied, "That's because Mrs. Madison loves everybody."[25]

Last Days as the President's Lady

In the fall of 1815, the Madisons moved from the Octagon House. They would live in the corner house of the Seven Buildings on Pennsylvania Avenue. After the war ended, America's merchants and farmers went back to work. The national economy was booming. American shipyards echoed with the noise of ships being built. Cargoes of trade goods were being shipped all over the world.

In 1817, James Madison's eight years as president came to an end. On March 4, the Madisons watched James Monroe take the oath of office. Monroe became the fifth president of the United States. Dolley and James prepared to leave Washington for Montpelier and retirement. It seemed the entire city was sad to see them go. The Madisons attended so many parties that they remained in Washington until April.

On April 6, Dolley and James Madison at last boarded a steamboat on the Potomac River. A friend, James K. Paulding, joined them on their journey home to Virginia. Paulding noticed how happy James Madison was to be going home. "During the voyage," Paulding described, "he was as a child; talked and joked with everybody on board, and reminded me of a schoolboy on a long vacation."[26] Dolley also looked forward to starting a new chapter in her life.

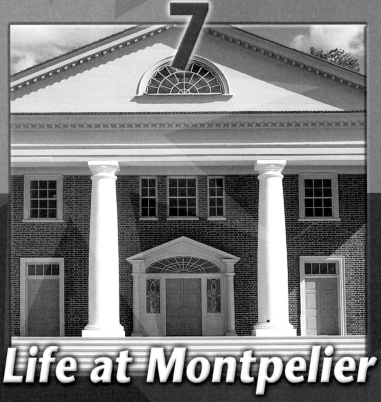

Life at Montpelier

"I wish, dearest, you had just such a country home as this," Dolley wrote to her sister Anna in Washington, "I truly believe it is the happiest and most true life."[1] The Madisons loved their home at Montpelier. When they arrived in 1817, James Madison was sixty-six years old, and Dolley would soon be forty-nine. Over the next nineteen years, the Madisons would spend most of their time on their country estate.

The Mansion

While James Madison was president, carpenters and bricklayers had been busy at Montpelier. By 1811, wings had been added to each end of the house. A grand new two-story roof covered the front porch. The original eight room house had become a twenty-two-room mansion.

The walls of the entrance hall were a bright, sunflower yellow color. The floor of the hall was covered with a colorful rug made in Venice, Italy. More than thirty pictures hung on the walls. These included pictures of the Madisons' personal friends, George Washington, John Adams, Thomas Jefferson, James Monroe, and Benjamin Franklin. Pictures of King Louis XVIII of France, Emperor Napoleon, an African king, and the Chinese philosopher Confucius hung there, too.[2] A visitor, Henry D. Gilpin, described that the hall had sofas on either side of the room. It also had "some large and good historical pictures by Flemish artists."[3]

Feeding Guests

In July 1820, Dolley wrote to her sister Anna Cutts, "Yesterday [July 4] we had ninety persons to dine with us at one table . . . on the lawn . . . "[4] The Madisons often held outside barbecues for dozens of guests in warm weather. Inside, formal meals in the dining room with two dozen guests were not unusual. Congress member George Ticknor once wrote that he had enjoyed at Montpelier "good soups, [meat,] fish and vegetables, well cooled—desert [*sic*] and excellent wines

While James Madison was president, he had a lot of work done on the Montpelier estate. He transformed it from an eight-room house to a twenty-two-room mansion. This is a view of the restored Montpelier estate today.

of various kinds." Margaret Bayard Smith remembered one morning meal: "We sat down between 15 and 20 persons to breakfast—and to a most excellent Virginian breakfast—tea, coffee, hot wheat bread, light cakes . . . corn loaf—cold ham, nice hashes, chickens, etc."[5]

During and after dinner, there was always good conversation. Dolley in her turban enjoyed her role as hostess. James Madison in small groups was a witty storyteller. The Madisons were wonderful hosts. One guest declared "They always made you glad to have come and sorry that you must go."[6]

Niece Mary Cutts later wrote, "Mr. Madison dearly loved and was proud of his wife . . . she was his solace and comfort, he could not bear her to leave his presence . . . " Dolley always seemed to know when her husband needed her. "If engaged in conversation," Mary Cutts added, "she would quickly rise and say, 'I must go to Madison.'"[7] Madison's health remained her greatest concern. In old age, James suffered from arthritis, stomach problems, colds, and flus.

Working Farmland

From the front door of Montpelier, one could see great green lawns. In the distance rose a view of the Blue Ridge Mountains. Montpelier was a place of peaceful beauty. The estate also contained much working farmland. Tobacco and wheat were the major crops. There was an excellent vegetable garden, and a mill for grinding grain, too. The Madisons also raised pigs, cattle, and sheep.

Four separate farms made up the estate, each with a little village of slave cabins. A visitor, Baron Montlezun,

Nelly Madison

When the Madisons returned to Montpelier in 1817, James's mother Nelly was eighty-six years old. She lived in her half of the mansion and had her own servants. James and Dolley visited her every afternoon. She could usually be found sitting on her sofa, knitting or reading. Dolley proved a loving daughter-in-law. One day Nelly Madison gazed at her and said, "You are my Mother now, and take care of me in my old age."[8]

recalled, "I went today to one of the farms of the President to see a wheat thrashing machine. . . . This machine turns out two hundred bushels a day." Montlezun described the special breed of sheep the Madisons raised. The sheep were called merinos, "the wool of which is highly prized and brings a good price."[9] Montlezun noticed that the cabins of the slaves "are very pretty, built of wood, clean, and comfortable."[10] Skilled slaves, including weavers, carpenters, and blacksmiths, kept the plantation running. Dolley kept busy organizing all of the meals each day for more than one hundred slaves.

Dolley and James both disliked slavery. But they believed that the Southern economy could not survive without slave workers. The Madisons treated their slaves well at Montpelier. James Madison's slave, Paul Jennings, later wrote, "Mr. Madison, I think was one of the best men that ever lived. I never . . . knew him to strike a slave. . . . Neither would he allow an overseer to do it."[11] Dolley often helped nurse sick slaves back to health with careful attention.

Payne Todd

"Everyone [asks] after you," Dolley once wrote to her son Payne Todd. "But, my dear son, it seems to be the wonder of them all that you should stay away from us for so long a time!"[12] Dolley's son had not grown into a responsible adult. He often disappeared from home. His behavior caused Dolley terrible heartache. She once wrote that Payne "comes not—nor do I hear from him, which covers me with sadness."[13]

Wherever he went, Payne got into trouble. He was a gambler and a drinker. He always needed money. James Madison secretly paid more than $20,000 to cover Payne's gambling debts. He did not want Dolley to know how bad things were. He paid an additional $20,000 that Dolley did know about, for a total of $40,000.

Twice, Payne was thrown into prison in Philadelphia, in 1829 and 1830, because he could not pay his bills. Dolley never lost faith in Payne, however. She remained a brave and forgiving mother. She always hoped for the best for her troubled son.

Joyful Dolley

Margaret Bayard Smith made a visit to Montpelier and Dolley asked her why she had not brought her young daughters along. Smith replied that she had not wanted her children to be a bother.

"Oh," laughed Dolley, "I should not have known they were here, among all the rest . . . " She explained that just then she had twenty-three guests staying at the house.

Smith exclaimed in surprise, "Why where do you store them?"

"Oh we have house room in plenty," smiled Dolley.[14]

Dolley often had grandnieces and grandnephews and other children stay with her. Her grandnephew, J. Madison Cutts Jr. remembered that "she always loved young children and was never happier than when they

White House Easters

According to legend, Payne Todd made a suggestion one day when he lived at the White House. Someplace he had heard or read about an egg hunt or roll. It was something the early Egyptians had done. Payne thought such a celebration would be great fun for children. Dolley liked the idea. She dyed hundreds of hard-boiled eggs in bright colors. On the Easter holiday, she invited neighborhood children to come and play with them. The yearly Easter Egg Hunt on the White House lawn is still a popular tradition.

gathered around her."[15] Margaret Bayard Smith realized, "She certainly has always been, and still is one of the happiest of human beings."[16]

Important Work

In 1824, Daniel Webster and George Ticknor visited Montpelier. They noticed that Dolley worked with James Madison each day, from ten in the morning until three o'clock in the afternoon. James Madison had kept careful notes when he was a member of the Constitutional Convention in 1787. Turning these notes into a history of the convention had become his main goal during retirement.

Madison's arthritis was a disease of his joints: ankles, knees, hips, wrists, elbows, even his knuckles. Sometimes he could hardly hold a pen. In December 1831, Dolley exclaimed to a niece, "his poor hands are still sore and so swollen as to be almost useless, and so I lend him mine."[17] Dolley worked as his secretary each day. She wrote when Madison could not. James liked wintertime the best.

> Dolley exclaimed to a niece, "his poor hands are still sore and so swollen as to be almost useless, and so I lend him mine."

In the winter, the Virginia roads were icy and muddy. Fewer visitors made the trip to Montpelier. As a result, he and Dolley had more free time to work on his papers. During his lifetime, three volumes describing the debates of the Constitutional Convention were prepared. They totaled about eighteen hundred pages.

Death of a President

By 1834, James Madison's arthritis was so painful he could hardly leave his bed. Dolley admitted she spent her days, "nursing and comforting my sick patient, who walks only from the bed in which he breakfasts to another."[18] As her husband's health grew worse, she explained that she had "never left him half an hour, for the last two years."[19]

Published after his death, James Madison's last public letter called "Advice to My Country" was written

Asher B. Durand painted this portrait of James Madison one year before his death. In his final years, James Madison suffered from arthritis, often keeping him in bed. Dolley always cared for him.

in Dolley's handwriting.[20] By June, it was clear he was nearing his end. On June 28, his niece Nelly Conway Madison Willis stood at his bedside. She saw that he was very uncomfortable.

"What is the matter, Uncle James?" she asked.

"Nothing more than a change of mind, my dear," Madison softly replied.[21]

His eyes closed. His head dropped. He stopped breathing. James Madison was dead at the age of eighty-five. He and Dolley had been married for nearly forty-two years. Sixty-eight-year-old Dolley Payne Todd Madison was once again a widow.

Chapter

8

First Lady of the Nation

The death of James Madison greatly saddened Americans. Already he was being called the "Father of the Constitution." The part he had played in creating the United States government had been great. Dolley buried her husband in the family graveyard at Montpelier. Day by day, she tried to control her sadness. By July, her niece Anna Payne reported, "She no longer gives way to the grief."[1] After her husband's death, Dolley wrote to her sister, "I have been as one in a troubled dream since my . . . loss of him."[2] In his will, James had left Dolley Montpelier, a house in Washington, and his writings.

Getting Published

"Especially do I value all his writings," Dolley declared.[3] Getting his papers published became her major wish. James Madison's written record of the Constitutional Convention preserved a great moment in American history. Dolley asked her son Payne to try to find a publisher for the papers. Payne was a poor choice for the job. By the end of 1836, Payne's many demands had ruined their chances with all of the large publishers.

Dolley had hoped the papers would be worth $100,000. In the end, it was Congress that offered to publish the first three volumes of Madison's papers. Congress agreed to pay $30,000. These volumes were published in 1840. James Madison had died owing money to friends and banks. He had borrowed to pay the costs of running Montpelier and for covering Payne Todd's many gambling debts. Dolley used the $30,000 to pay off these expenses and to give gifts to charities and family members.

Return to Washington

At the age of sixty-nine, in the fall of 1837, Dolley chose to move to the Cutts House in Washington. Her niece Anna Payne came with her. She planned to spend winters in Washington and summers at Montpelier.

She left Payne Todd in charge of Montpelier. The Cutts House was a two-story building on Lafayette Square near the White House. Dolley's brother-in-law Richard Cutts had built the house in 1818, but Dolley owned it.

In Washington, Dolley was warmly welcomed back. She instantly received invitations to dinners, parties, and balls. Everyone wanted to visit her. One of Dolley's first callers in Lafayette Square was ex-President John Quincy Adams. Senator Daniel Webster, General Winfield Scott, and President Martin Van Buren also stopped by to greet her. "Mrs. Madison," exclaimed Van Buren after one of her parties, "is the most brilliant hostess this country has ever known."[4] On New Year's Day, July 4, and other holidays, her house was always crowded.

Unable to afford new clothes, Dolley continued to wear her old ones. She refused to be embarrassed. The dress she wore most often was a black velvet gown with loose sleeves and a full skirt. It had a very low neckline filled in with white cloth that rose to her neck. On her head, she usually wore a white satin turban. Around her shoulders she often draped a bright satin scarf. After Philip Hone met Dolley, he remarked, "She is a young lady of [eighty] years and upward, [who] goes to parties and receives company like the 'Queen of this New World.'"[5]

Before his death, James Madison had already begun selling off some of the land at Montpelier. When he needed money, Payne Todd sold pieces of the furniture. In 1840, Dolley was forced to sell some Montpelier land to a Virginia merchant named Henry Moncure.

By 1844, she sadly realized she had to sell the rest of the Montpelier estate to Moncure, including the mansion and the slaves.

The *Princeton* Tragedy

Dolley was as well known in the capital as the President of the United States. Members of the House of Representatives always gave her a seat, which she could take whenever she visited. Such a high honor had never been granted to anyone before.

On February 28, 1844, Dolley accepted a special invitation. She joined other guests on a fifteen-mile trip aboard the United States warship *Princeton*. President John Tyler, cabinet members, and important navy officers were also aboard.

Montpelier Today

Between 1844 and 1901, Montpelier had six different owners. In 1901, wealthy William DuPont Sr. bought the property. When his daughter Marion DuPont Scott died in 1983, she deeded Montpelier to the National Trust for Historic Preservation. That organization opened Montpelier to the public in 1987. In recent years, an expensive restoration has returned the house to the way it looked when the Madisons lived there.

The *Princeton* carried a giant cannon called "The Peacemaker." It was the navy's newest weapon. It had been fired successfully more than once during the trip. When it was fired opposite Fort Washington, however, it suddenly exploded. Chunks of iron flew in all directions. Secretary of State Abel P. Upshur, Secretary of the Navy Thomas W. Gilmer, and Navy Captain Beverly Kennon instantly fell killed. Other bleeding people lay moaning on the deck.

Dolley rushed to help the wounded. By chance, she had escaped harm. All of the ladies had been on a lower deck at the time of the deadly explosion.

A New Invention

On May 24, 1844, Samuel F. B. Morse asked Dolley to attend the first public test of his new invention, the telegraph. In the Supreme Court room of the Capitol, one telegraph key had been set up. Forty miles away, in Baltimore, Maryland, another had been placed in a railroad station warehouse. A telegraph wire stretched the entire distance between. As a witness to the grand experiment, Dolley heard the first message ever to be sent by telegraph. The words were a quote from the Bible "What hath God wrought?"

The test was a total success. The message was clearly received. Morse next turned to Dolley. He asked if she wanted to send a message. Dolley knew that a Baltimore cousin of hers, the wife of congress member John Wethered, was present at the other end of the line. Dolley asked that Morse send the following: "Message

Dolley Madison was aboard the Princeton when its new weapon, "The Peacemaker," exploded. Dolley was able to help some of the wounded.

from Mrs. Madison. She sends her love to Mrs. Wethered."[6] Dolley's was the first personal message ever sent by telegraph.

Help from Congress

On May 20, 1848, Dolley's eightieth birthday, Congress voted to buy the rest of James Madison's writings. Dolley was paid $25,000 for the last four volumes. The first payment helped Dolley pay off her debts and Payne Todd's debts, too. Dolley had enough money now on which she could live.

Dolley helped raise money to build the Washington Monument. She watched the ceremony as a special guest, when the cornerstone was laid on July 4, 1848. New Yorker William Kemble remembered meeting her

A Loyal Servant

A lack of money continued to trouble Dolley in her later years. In about 1840, Dolley had sold family slave Paul Jennings to her Washington neighbor, Senator Daniel Webster, who had promised that Jennings could earn his freedom. Jennings remembered, "When I was a servant to Mr. Webster, he often sent me to her with a market-basket full of [food], and told me whenever I saw anything in the house that I thought she was in need of, to take it to her. I often did this, and [sometimes] gave her small sums from my own pocket."[7] In 1847, Paul Jennings did earn his freedom from Daniel Webster.

around that time. "The old lady is a very hearty, good looking woman. . . . Soon after we were seated, we [were] on the most friendly terms."[8]

At the end of his term as president, James K. Polk planned one last party at the White House. He invited Dolley to be his special guest. On February 7, 1849, she proudly took her place in the East Room of the White House. Dolley smiled as the Marine Band started playing. President Polk entered the outer hall of the White House and the party began. "Towards the close of the evening," President Polk later wrote in his diary, "I passed through the crowded rooms with . . . Mrs. Madison on my arm."[9]

Dolley Madison was a special guest when the cornerstone of the Washington Monument was laid on July 4, 1848. The Washington Monument still stands in the National Mall in Washington, D.C.

"Yes, and I Love You"

In the spring of 1849, Dolley's health began to fail. To an old friend, she wrote, "I rose this morning with the sun, and felt as if I could fly with the aid of a sweet breeze . . . but now, at 10 o'clock I am . . . ready for a nap."[10] On July 8, 1849, she was so weak she stayed in bed. Once, a niece came to her bedside with a personal problem.

Dolley told her, "My dear, do not trouble yourself about it, there is nothing in this world worth caring for."

The niece wondered, "Aunt, you who have lived so long, do you think so?"

"Yes!" Dolley repeated, "believe me, I who have lived in it so long, repeat to you that there is nothing in it worth caring for."[11]

As the days passed, Dolley's friend Eliza Collins came and sat at her bedside. Collins later described that Dolley would sometimes wake up. She would "smile her long smile, put out her arms to [hug] those whom she loved and were near her, then gently [fall asleep again]." Once she opened her eyes. Eliza Collins asked if she knew who she was. "Do I know you, my dear Betsey," Dolley weakly replied, "—Yes, and I love you."[12]

Dolley Payne Todd Madison died on the evening of July 12, 1849, at the age of eighty-one. Mourners paid their respects at the house on Lafayette Square. On July 16, her body was moved. Her coffin lay in St. John's Episcopal Church. Hundreds of saddened people came to say good-bye to the woman they loved.

On the day of her funeral, all government offices in Washington were closed. President Zachary Taylor, the cabinet, Congress members, and Supreme Court justices, marched behind the casket. Dolley Madison's funeral was the largest ever held in Washington up to that time. At first, Dolley's body was kept at the Congressional Cemetery. In 1858, family members moved her remains to Montpelier to rest next to her husband's in the family graveyard.

A daguerreotype of Dolley Madison taken in the last years of her life by famous photographer Mathew Brady.

Famous Dolley

Dolley Madison was famous in her own lifetime. After her death, her fame continued. Over the years, some companies have thought that her name would help sell their products. Her first name has been spelled wrong, but there have been The Dolly Madison Wine Fruit Industries, Dolly Madison Popcorn, The Dolly Madison Bakery, The Dolly Madison Dairy, and Dolly Madison Ice Cream. Companies have manufactured Dolly Madison china, dolls, and even cigars.

Gifts to a Nation

After Dolley Madison died, according to legend, at her funeral President Zachary Taylor eulogized her as the "First Lady." This may have been the first time that this title was used in connection with the president's wife.[13] No record of President Taylor's eulogy still exists, but the term "First Lady" has been used to describe the President's wife ever since. Dolley Madison contributed much to America's history during her long life.

During her Quaker childhood, Dolley Madison learned about the value of hard work, simple joys, equality, and social justice. As a young woman in Philadelphia, she witnessed the revolution and the birth of American democracy. Always, Dolley was full of good cheer and kindness. She did her best to spread these feelings to others.

Her marriage to James Madison in 1794 brought Dolley into the world of national politics. As the wife of an important congress member, she learned how to entertain and make a good impression. These skills would prove to be very valuable. James Madison was quiet and thoughtful in large groups. Dolley was outspoken and charming. Her good-natured spirit helped promote Madison's political ideas.

In 1801, Dolley arrived in Washington, D.C. as the wife of the secretary of state. The capital was a new, unformed city. Dolley went to work to help give it character. She became President Jefferson's unofficial hostess. She made guests relaxed and comfortable at White House dinners. She became a fashion leader, too, trying new styles of clothes. She found ways to include women in Washington politics and society.

In 1808, James Madison ran for president. He remained silent and in the background during the campaign. Dolley, however, gave dinners and speeches to help win her husband valuable support. In the end, Madison won the election. Many people agreed Dolley had played an important part in his victory.

As the president's wife, Dolley gained more influence than ever before. She decorated the White House. She made it a place of which Americans could truly be proud. Her weekly White House parties drew people from all over the country. She encouraged the exchange of political ideas among Republicans and Federalists, between men and women. One of Dolley's

James (front) and Dolley Madison's gravestones in the family graveyard at Montpelier.

warm smiles, or a simple gentle word from her, could calm an argument or win a friend. "How kind is this woman," Margaret Bayard Smith once remarked. "How can any human being be her enemy."[14]

Above all, Dolley Madison is famous for being a national hero. During the War of 1812, Americans looked to Dolley for hope. She never lost her faith that the country would survive its difficult challenge. Her personal bravery has become legendary. She saved the famous White House painting of George Washington. She escaped Washington with a few hours to spare. After the British burned the White House, she returned. She refused to admit defeat. She vowed that the president's home and the capital would be rebuilt. She became a lasting symbol of America's strength and hardiness.

In retirement, Dolley made beautiful Montpelier a place of welcome to visitors. Her help in editing her husband's papers guaranteed James Madison's fame as "The Father of the Constitution." During the years of her old age, Dolley returned to Washington. She missed the excitement of the capital, and she happily took part in many of the city's social and political events.

When Dolley died in 1849, many Americans felt they had lost a personal friend. Her niece, Mary Cutts, had once said, "Those who knew her best, loved her most."[15] For more than fifty years, Dolley Madison played a great role in America's history.

CHRONOLOGY

1768 —**May 20:** Dolley is born in New Garden, North Carolina.

1769 —Returns with family to Virginia.

1783 —Moves with family to Philadelphia.

1790 —**January 7:** Marries John Todd Jr.

1793 —**Summer and fall:** Yellow fever sweeps through Philadelphia.

—**October 24:** Her husband and son, William, die of the fever.

1794 —**May:** Meets Congress member James Madison.

—**September 15:** She and Madison marry.

1797–

1801 —Retires with Madison to Montpelier, Virginia.

1801–

1809 —James Madison serves as secretary of state; Dolley serves as President Thomas Jefferson's White House hostess. She sets national examples in fashion and manners.

1809–

1817 —James Madison serves as President of the United States. As the president's wife, Dolley is at the center of Washington, D.C. society. She decorates the White House and holds regular open house parties.

1812–

1814 —The War of 1812 fought between the United States and Great Britain.

1814 —**August 24:** Dolley saves White House valuables and escapes Washington. Invading British troops set fire to the White House and the Capitol.

—**December 24:** Treaty of Ghent is signed.

1817–

1836 —In retirement at Montpelier; Dolley helps edit James Madison's Constitutional Convention papers.

1836 —**June 28:** James Madison dies of heart failure.

1837 —Dolley returns to Washington to live part-time.

1844 —Sells Montpelier estate.

—**February 28:** Present at the *Princeton* warship tragedy.

—**May 24:** Sends the first personal telegraph message.

1849 —**July 12:** Dies at the age of eighty-one.

CHAPTER NOTES

CHAPTER 1
The Escape From Washington

1. Ethel Stephens Arnett, *Mrs. James Madison: The Incomparable Dolley* (Greensboro, N.C.: Piedmont Press, 1972), p. 240.
2. Richard N. Cote, *Strength and Honor: The Life of Dolley Madison* (Mount Pleasant, S.C.: Corinthian Books, 2005), pp. 4–5.
3. Ibid., p. 12.
4. Arnett, p. 240.
5. Catherine Allgor, *A Perfect Union: Dolley Madison and the Creation of the American Nation* (New York: Henry Holt and Company, 2006), p. 313.
6. Cote, p. 296.
7. Ibid., p. 297.
8. Allgor, p. 4.
9. Arnett, p. 240.

CHAPTER 2
A Quaker Childhood

1. Richard N. Cote, *Strength and Honor: The Life of Dolley Madison* (Mount Pleasant, S.C.: Corinthian Books, 2005), p. 39.
2. Ibid., p. 32.
3. Ethel Stephens Arnett, *Mrs. James Madison: The Incomparable Dolley* (Greensboro, N.C.: Piedmont Press, 1972), p. 6.
4. Cote, p. 49.
5. Ibid., p. 64.

6. Catherine Allgor, *A Perfect Union: Dolley Madison and the Creation of the American Nation* (New York: Henry Holt and Company, 2006), p. 19.
7. Ibid.
8. Ibid., pp. 19–20.
9. Robert A. Rutland, *James Madison and the Search for Nationhood* (Washington, D.C.: The Library of Congress, 1981), p. 56.
10. Allgor, p. 22.

CHAPTER 3
The Great Little Madison

1. Richard N. Cote, *Strength and Honor: The Life of Dolley Madison* (Mount Pleasant, S.C.: Corinthian Books, 2005), p. 96.
2. Ibid., p. 97.
3. Ethel Stephens Arnett, *Mrs. James Madison: The Incomparable Dolley* (Greensboro, N.C.: Piedmont Press, 1972), p. 49.
4. Catherine Allgor, *A Perfect Union: Dolley Madison and the Creation of the American Nation* (New York: Henry Holt and Company, 2006), p. 25.
5. Paul F. Boller, *Presidential Wives* (New York: Oxford University Press, 1988), p. 37.
6. Ibid.
7. Arnett, pp. 58–59.
8. Merrill D. Peterson, ed., *The Founding Father, James Madison, A Biography in His Own Words* (New York: Newsweek Books, 1974), vol. 2, pp. 250–251.
9. Cote, pp. 114–115.
10. Boller, p. 44.
11. Arnett, p. 61.
12. Irving Brant, *The Fourth President, A Life of James Madison* (Indianapolis: The Bobbs-Merrill Company, 1970), p. 278.
13. Cote, p. 128.
14. Arnett, p. 131.

15. Boller, p. 38.
16. Arnett, p. 75.
17. Cote, p. 192.
18 Ibid., p. 188.

CHAPTER 4
The President's Hostess

1. Catherine Allgor, *A Perfect Union: Dolley Madison and the Creation of the American Nation* (New York: Henry Holt and Company, 2006), p. 48.
2. James Parton, "The Presidential Election of 1800," *The Atlantic Online*, originally published in *The Atlantic Monthly*, July 1873, <http://www.theatlantic.com/politics/policamp/parton.htm> (August 4, 2009).
3. Ethel Stephens Arnett, *Mrs. James Madison: The Incomparable Dolley* (Greensboro, N.C.: Piedmont Press, 1972), p. 134.
4. Ibid., p. 140.
5. Allgor, p. 50.
6. Paul F. Boller, *Presidential Wives* (New York: Oxford University Press, 1988), p. 39.
7. Allgor, p. 105.
8. Richard N. Cote, *Strength and Honor: The Life of Dolley Madison* (Mount Pleasant, S.C.: Corinthian Books, 2005), p. 201.
9. Arnett, p. 158.
10. Allgor, p. 73.
11. Cote, p. 321.
12. Allgor, p. 60.
13. Catherine Allgor, *Parlor Politics* (Charlottesville, Va.: University Press of Virginia, 2000), p. 37.
14. Cote, p. 224.
15. Ibid., p. 223.
16. Diana Dixon Healy, *America's First Ladies* (New York: Atheneum, 1988), p. 20.
17. Cote, p. 241.
18. Arnett, p. 78.

19. Allgor, *A Perfect Union*, p. 112.
20. Arnett, p. 79.
21. Allgor, p. 129.
22. Ibid., pp. 117–118.
23. Allgor, *Parlor Politics*, p. 71.
24. Allgor, *A Perfect Union*, p. 129.
25. Boller, pp. 45–46.
26. Ibid., p. 38.

CHAPTER 5
Queen Dolley

1. Merrill D. Peterson, ed., *The Founding Father, James Madison, A Biography in His Own Words* (New York: Newsweek Books, 1974), vol. 2, p. 274.
2. Ethel Stephens Arnett, *Mrs. James Madison: The Incomparable Dolley* (Greensboro, N.C.: Piedmont Press, 1972), p. 163.
3. Richard N. Cote, *Strength and Honor: The Life of Dolley Madison* (Mount Pleasant, S.C.: Corinthian Books, 2005), pp. 257–258.
4. Ibid., p. 258.
5. Ibid., p. 260.
6. Catherine Allgor, *Parlor Politics* (Charlottesville, Va.: University Press of Virginia, 2000), p. 93.
7. Catherine Allgor, *A Perfect Union: Dolley Madison and the Creation of the American Nation* (New York: Henry Holt and Company, 2006), p. 160.
8. Allgor, *Parlor Politics*, p. 61.
9. Allgor, *A Perfect Union*, p. 167.
10. Ibid., pp. 173–174.
11. Ibid.
12. Diana Dixon Healy, *America's First Ladies* (New York: Atheneum, 1988), p. 21.
13. Allgor, *Parlor Politics*, p. 78.
14. Allgor, *A Perfect Union*, p. 240.

15. Paul M. Zall, *America's First Ladies*, ed. Robert P. Watson (Pasadena, Calif.: Salem Press, Inc., 2002), p. 38.
16. Allgor, p. 174.
17. Allgor, *Parlor Politics*, p. 94.
18. Allgor, *A Perfect Union*, p. 249.
19. Ibid., p. 250.
20. Ibid., p. 245.
21. Ibid., p. 184.
22. Cote, p. 227.
23. Allgor, pp. 258–259.

CHAPTER 6
Mr. Madison's War

1. Harold S. Schultz, *James Madison* (New York: Twayne Publishers, Inc., 1970), p. 154.
2. Paul F. Boller, *Presidential Wives* (New York: Oxford University Press, 1988), p. 42.
3. Kenneth W. Leish, ed., *The American Heritage Pictorial History of the Presidents of the United States* (New York: American Heritage Publishing Co., Inc., 1968), vol. I, p. 132.
4. Dolley Madison, "From Dolley Payne Madison to Anna Cutts, 20 March 1812," *The Dolley Madison Project*, letter dated March 20, 1812, n.d., <http://www2.vcdh.virginia.edu/madison/exhibit/washington/letters/032012.html> (August 3, 2009).
5. Catherine Allgor, *A Perfect Union: Dolley Madison and the Creation of the American Nation* (New York: Henry Holt and Company, 2006), pp. 288–289.
6. Ethel Stephens Arnett, *Mrs. James Madison: The Incomparable Dolley* (Greensboro, N.C.: Piedmont Press, 1972), p. 213.
7. Catherine Allgor, *Parlor Politics* (Charlottesville, Va.: University Press of Virginia, 2000), p. 90.

8. Richard N. Cote, *Strength and Honor: The Life of Dolley Madison* (Mount Pleasant, S.C.: Corinthian Books, 2005), p. 291.
9. William A. DeGregorio, *The Complete Book of U.S. Presidents* (New York: Dembner Books, 1984), p. 66.
10. Cote, p. 281.
11. Lucia Beverly Cutts, ed., *Memoirs and Letters of Dolly Madison: Wife of James Madison, President of the United States* (Boston: Houghton, Mifflin and Company, 1887), p. 93.
12. Allgor, *A Perfect Union*, p. 2.
13. Ibid., p. 311.
14. Cote, p. 307.
15. Ibid., pp. 304–305.
16. J. Thomas Scharf, *History of Maryland From the Earliest Period to the Present Day*, vol. III (Baltimore: John B. Piet, 1879), p. 89.
17. Allgor, p. 317.
18. Ibid., p. 320.
19. Cote, p. 313.
20. Boller, p. 43.
21. Cote, p. 312.
22. Allgor, pp. 332–333.
23. Ibid., p. 342.
24. Allgor, *Parlor Politics*, pp. 97–98.
25. Arnett, p. 253.
26. Brant, p. 607.

CHAPTER 7
Life at Montpelier

1. Lucia Beverly Cutts, ed., *Memoirs and Letters of Dolly Madison: Wife of James Madison, President of the United States* (Boston: Houghton, Mifflin and Company, 1887), p. 174.
2. Richard N. Cote, *Strength and Honor: The Life of Dolley Madison* (Mount Pleasant, S.C.: Corinthian Books, 2005), pp. 185–186.

3. Matthew G. Hyland, *Montpelier and the Madisons* (Charleston, S.C.: History Press, 2007), pp. 72–73.

4. Ethel Stephens Arnett, *Mrs. James Madison: The Incomparable Dolley* (Greensboro, N.C.: Piedmont Press, 1972), p. 310.

5. Cote, pp. 272, 332.

6. Arnett, p. 310.

7. "Reading 3: James and Dolley Madison at Montpelier," *Memories of Montpelier*, National Park Service, from *Mary Cutts Memoir*, Cutts Collection, Library of Congress, n.d., <http://www.nps.gov/nr/twhp/wwwlps/lessons/46montpelier/46facts3.htm> (August 4, 2009).

8. Cote, p. 330.

9. Hyland, p. 79.

10. Ibid., p. 82.

11. Arnett, p. 73.

12. Cutts, p. 167.

13. Catherine Allgor, *A Perfect Union: Dolley Madison and the Creation of the American Nation* (New York: Henry Holt and Company, 2006), p. 351.

14. Cote, p. 271.

15. Arnett, p. 254.

16. Ibid., p. 302.

17. Allen Culling Clark, *Life and Letters of Dolly Madison* (Washington, D.C.: Press of W. F. Roberts Co., 1914), p. 244.

18. Cutts, p. 193.

19. Allgor, p. 374.

20. Paul F. Boller, *Presidential Wives* (New York: Oxford University Press, 1988), p. 43.

21. Merrill D. Peterson, ed., *The Founding Father, James Madison, A Biography in His Own Words* (New York: Newsweek Books, 1974), vol. 2, p. 405.

CHAPTER 8
First Lady of the Nation

1. Catherine Allgor, *A Perfect Union: Dolley Madison and the Creation of the American Nation* (New York: Henry Holt and Company, 2006), p. 378.
2. Matthew G. Hyland, *Montpelier and the Madisons* (Charleston, S.C.: History Press, 2007), p. 90.
3. Allgor, p. 379.
4. Paul F. Boller, *Presidential Wives* (New York: Oxford University Press, 1988), p. 43.
5. Bayard Tuckerman, ed., *The Diary of Philip Hone, 1825–1851* (New York: Dodd, Mead and Company, 1889), p. 121.
6. Boller, p. 48.
7. Richard N. Cote, *Strength and Honor: The Life of Dolley Madison* (Mount Pleasant, S.C.: Corinthian Books, 2005), pp. 355–356.
8. Ibid., p. 349.
9. Ibid., p. 341.
10. Allgor, p. 397.
11. Ibid., p. 398.
12. Ibid.
13. "First Lady Biography: Dolley Madison," *National First Ladies' Library*, 2009, <http://www.firstladies.org/biographies/firstladies.aspx?biography=4> (August 4, 2009).
14. Cote, p. 272.
15. Ethel Stephens Arnett, *Mrs. James Madison: The Incomparable Dolley* (Greensboro, N.C.: Piedmont Press, 1972), p. 330.

GLOSSARY

ambassador—An official representative to a foreign country.

Articles of Confederation—The first set of laws governing the United States of America.

burgess—A person chosen to represent Virginians in its colonial government.

commission—A group of people given the power to act for others.

consul—A chief judge.

delegate—A person acting for, or representing, others.

epidemic—A sudden outbreak of disease.

escort—To go with or give company.

eulogize—To speak or write in high praise, most often at a funeral after a person dies.

inaugural—The ceremony that marks the start of a person's time in office.

macaw—A colorful parrot of Central or South America.

overseer—A farm manager.

patent—A grant giving an inventor all rights to make, use, or sell an invention for a certain period of time.

restoration—Returning something to the way it was before.

FURTHER READING

Books

Childress, Diana. *The War of 1812.* Minneapolis, Minn.: Lerner Publications Co., 2004.

Madison, Dolley. *The Selected Letters of Dolley Payne Madison.* Edited by David B. Mattern and Holly C. Shulman. Charlottesville, VA.: University of Virginia Press, 2003.

Santella, Andrew. *James Madison.* Mankato, Minn.: Compass Point Books, 2003.

Weatherly, Myra. *Dolley Madison: America's First Lady.* Greensboro, N.C.: Morgan Reynolds Pub., 2003.

Witteman, Barbara. *Dolley Madison: First Lady.* Mankato, Minn.: Bridgestone Books, 2003.

Internet Addresses

The Dolley Madison Project: The Life, Letters, and Legacy of Dolley Payne Madison

<http://www2.vcdh.virginia.edu/madison/index.html>

Eyewitness to History.com: "The British Burn Washington, D.C., 1814"

<http://www.eyewitnesstohistory.com/washingtonsack.htm>

National First Ladies' Library—Dolley Madison

<http://www.firstladies.org/biographies/firstladies.aspx?biography=4>

INDEX